The Food Traveler's Guide to Emilia Romagna

THE FOOD TRAVELER'S GUIDE TO EMILIA ROMAGNA

How to taste the history and tradition of Italy

Amber Hoffman

With Husband In Tow Publishing

CONTENTS

WHAT PEOPLE
ARE SAYING

This book is the perfect travel companion for those who want to eat their way through Emilia Romagna. But it's so much more than just an informational guide: it's for any food and wine lover who wants a deeper understanding about Italian products. You can practically taste the delicately sliced tartufo and ricotta-stuffed cappelletti through the pages!

- Annette White, Chef and Owner of Sugo Trattoria and Author of "Bucket List Adventures"

I met Amber (and her husband, Eric) during their second "official" visit to Emilia Romagna—the visit that made them fall in love with the region and the food here. I honestly have never met someone that is not from the region who is as passionate about the food and wine as Amber. The fact that she truly cares about every single detail of her food and wine discoveries is a guarantee that what you read in this book will be the best way for you to go and experience Emilia Romagna to the fullest!

- Nick Montemaggi, iambassador and #EuroFoodTrip campaign

"The bible to discovering Emilia Romagna through food and wine!"

- Nelson Carvalheiro, Author of "The Portuguese Travel Cookbook"

This is the essential guide book for anyone going to Emilia Romagna, but especially a food and wine focused traveller. I only wish I had a book like this before my first visit to Emilia Romagna. This book is all you need to make your trip a perfect one.

- Akasha Richmond, Restauranteur, chef, and owner of AR Cucina, Los Angeles

I was hooked on this book from the beginning. What I thought would be merely a food and wine book became a complete experience for all my senses: I could smell the Parmigiano cheese, taste the balsamic vinegar, and feel the passion of the people. If food was a religion, Amber would be the bishop—she seems to know every detail of every single corner of Emilia Romagna's gastronomy, then spreads it on the pages of this book with professionalism, personal opinions, and love. I have been to Emilia Romagna on several occasions, but now I can't wait to return to discover it from a completely different angle.

- Jaume Marin, Marketing Director, Costa Brava Tourism and #EuroFoodTrip campaign

GRAZIE MILLE!

I never thought I could write a book on Italian food, that I would come to know so much about it and then be able to share my knowledge. In order to accomplish that seemingly impossible task, I have to thank my many Italian guides and experts who helped Eric and me explore Emilia Romagna over the last few years—Helena, Nick, and Silvia, to name just a few.

And, of course, thank you to "The Husband In Tow," who helped me scarf down all the food and gulp down all the wine that was necessary to make this book happen. It was a true sacrifice, I know…

PREFACE

I am not Italian. I do not speak Italian fluently. I do not profess to be an Italian gastronome or a *sommelier*.

Yet, as an American, I speak with people who live in Emilia Romagna, and they are impressed with my knowledge of the region. I've been taught well. I've been called a budding expert on Emilia Romagna. Let's hope that is the case.

This book is a culinary travel guide to Emilia Romagna. Culinary travel guides are more than just restaurant guides. They share the stories behind the food: the chefs, the winemakers, and even the ingredients. They are meant to inspire people to get out there and travel, and to explore a destination in a unique way.

But, these guides also provide specific recommendations, such as which foods to track down when exploring a new destination, which food markets to explore, and where to go eat all of this amazing food.

This culinary travel guide might not cover every DOP or IGP product, but it does explain what those terms mean. It might not list every restaurant in the region, but it does offer solid recommendations. It might not list every wine it is possible to drink, but it does explain the main wines of the region and how to taste them.

I hope to provide a foundational roadmap to explore Emilia Romagna. To that end, this book includes recommendations for what and where to eat across the region, with a focus on Modena and Bologna: two of the most popular cities. I've also shared stories of the food producers, winemakers, and chefs who lie at the center of the food capital of Italy.

INTRODUCTION

I love Italian food. I grew up in New Jersey, with a pizzeria on every corner and Italian Christmas Eve dinners with trays of lasagna and baked ziti. Early trips to Italy included searches for the type of Italian food I grew up eating. As I came to discover, the Italian comfort food found in the United States is predominantly from the south—from Naples, Sicily, and Calabria, where many Italian-American immigrants hailed from.

Over the 15-plus years I've spent traveling to Italy, almost all of it had been to Rome and the north. I've traveled to Rome, Florence, and Venice. All over Tuscany and Umbria. Lucca, Siena, San Gimignano, Cortona, Orvieto, and Assisi, with, a quick trip to Bologna. Into Piedmont, Turin, Genoa, Asti, and little seaside towns like Camogli. One New Years Eve was spent in Milan. Those annual trips to Italy involved drinking Chianti and scarfing down as many plates of *pappardelle al cinghiale* as I could.

After a three year hiatus from traveling to Italy, I felt the itch to return. We were living in Southeast Asia at the time, but felt a need to gorge on the Italian specialties we were sheltered from in Asia.

Our immediate thoughts turned to Tuscany and Umbria because many of our best trips involved the hill towns and wineries that sprinkled central Italy. Then we watched an episode of Anthony Bourdain's "No Reservations." Perhaps I owe this book all to him, but please don't feed his ego.

We were living in Bali. I was working at the kitchen table of our Ubud villa, editing a book for another author. Eric started playing the episode where Bourdain tours Emilia Romagna, a region I had never really heard of before. Of course I had heard of Modena. And, we've been to Bologna before. It was an awful trip.

Our first trip to Bologna was in the winter of 2010. Prior to Bologna, we had a lovely stay with Italian friends in Lucca. They took us to some of their favorite countryside eateries. We walked the old stone walls around the city. We drank coffee in the large *piazze*, or squares, of Lucca. They asked if we could stay longer, but we had already booked a hotel in Bologna. We couldn't cancel. We left. We regretted it immediately.

It was grey, cold, and rainy in Bologna. The general weather of the winter months. Our hotel was a little impersonal, but centrally located. We wandered around eating Bolognese cuisine, drinking red wine, and downing platters of cured meats and cheeses.

It was *fine*, but I felt as though we were missing something. I did no research ahead of time. I did not Google culinary travel blogs, or even search on TripAdvisor. We just wandered, ate a few meals, shivered in the damp cold, and wished we stayed in Lucca.

At the time of that first trip, I had no idea Bologna was in Emilia Romagna, or what that meant. I had no idea what was just outside the city limits, along the *Via Emilia*.

Back to Bourdain. At first, the episode just played in the background, along with Eric's occasional groans of starvation and jealousy, as we lived on a Hindu island, in a Muslim country, with little access to good Italian wine, and merely passable options for Italian cuisine.

I quickly became distracted from my book editing. I started to pay more attention to the episode.

Just watching Bourdain gorge on plates of pasta at a balsamic vinegar producer near Modena, down bottles of Italian wine, and devour cured meats I had never heard of, I was hooked. There is a slight chance that I started to drool all over my laptop, and all attempts at book editing that night were entirely abandoned. Before the end of the episode, I was sitting next to Eric on the sofa Googling "Emilia Romagna".

We made the decision that night: Our next trip to Italy would be to explore Emilia Romagna. After three years of noticeable absence, we finally returned to Italy, to Emilia Romagna, that fall. We returned three additional times in the following 18 months.

During our first visit, I knew I wanted to write a book about the region. Although the topic of that book is different than this one (and perhaps will become my second book on the region), I knew I had to share more about the food and wine of the area. Not only is Emilia Romagna home to some of the most notable food products in Europe, but there is a passion that underlies eating that only exists in a handful of places.

When researching this book, I came across an advertisement on the website for the consortium of *mortadella* producers. It was an old poster, from 1935, advertising *"La Settimana Della Cucina,"* essentially, the week of food. Presumably this was a food festival held in Bologna, in 1935! It just proves that the Italians in Emilia Romagna have been celebrating food for way longer than the existence of Restaurant Weeks across major cities. This history of celebrating food is what I hope to capture in this book.

MAP OF EMILIA ROMAGNA

Courtesy of Emilia Romagna Tourism

PART I

THE PRODUCTS OF EMILIA ROMAGNA

When it comes to tourism in Italy, there's a holy trinity of cities: Rome, Florence, and Venice. During a second trip, a tourist might start to explore outside the major cities, perhaps leading to a trip around Tuscany—exploring hill towns, tasting the Super Tuscan wines, and living out their own version of "Under the Tuscan Sun." Next, maybe, is a visit to Cinque Terre to explore seaside hill towns dotted with brightly painted row houses. A tourist of Italian-American descent might travel south to trace their heritage.

All Italian destinations are fabulous in their own right: they offer history, culture, and beautiful scenery. And the food is often good, even if it *is* sometimes hard to find authentic meals in touristy spots like Rome and Venice.

But for true foodies, Emilia Romagna is the only logical destination.

1

WHAT IS EMILIA ROMAGNA?

Emilia Romagna is a large region that reaches from Rimini on the east coast almost to Milan towards the west. It encompasses Bologna (home of *lasagne*), Modena (home of traditional balsamic vinegar), Parma (known for its *prosciutto* ham), and Reggio-Emilia (which gives its name to *Parmigiano Reggiano*). There's also a little town to the west called Piacenza, which is home to *pancetta*. Then there's white truffles, pasta, and gelato too!

Emilia Romagna is one of the best culinary travel experiences for any so-called foodie. There is so much history and tradition surrounding food. New and exciting restaurants mixed with generations old farms and family-owned food factories. And, as of 2016, home to the best restaurant in the world.

So, why is it that so few people travel to Emilia Romagna?

Until recently, many travelers had never even heard of the region. They may be familiar with Bologna, Modena, or Parma.

But, marketing Emilia Romagna has been a bit of a struggle as the region has had a bit of an identity crisis, as formally there were the two regions: Emilia and Romagna. To this day, residents continue to identify themselves as *Emiliano* or *Romagnolo*. Believe it or not, it's fairly easy to tell the difference by looking at what wine they drink daily: Lambrusco or Pignoletto for the former, and Sangiovese or Albana for the latter.

In recent years, the government of Emilia Romagna has focused on unique ways to promote the region to increase tourism, particularly related to food. In 2016, Chef Massimo Bottura's Osteria Francescana was named the #1 restaurant in the world, beating out Girona's El Celler Can Roca. There is even a food amusement park in the works. But once a traveler starts to eat in Emilia Romagna, it becomes clear that it should be a region on the culinary map as one of the gastronomic capitals of the world.

Why Food in Emilia Romagna is So Good – DOP and IGP

The slow food movement is taking off all over the world, along with a growing appreciation for where our food comes from and what goes into producing quality food. People everywhere are embracing the concept of farm-to-table cuisine. In Emilia Romagna, though, they've been focused on farm-to-table, quality food for decades and through many generations. There is also a focus on tradition, and of understanding the history of a food product, or a dish, so as not to lose traditional flavors and to maintain traditional techniques.

A series of consortia are responsible for maintaining food quality in Italy. They provide labels to guarantee that certain products are from a specific geographical location and are produced according to strict traditional guidelines. This is common across Europe, but in Italy, these products are known as DOP (*Denominazione Origine Protetta*) and IGP (*Indicazione Geografica Protetta*). There is a third category for food classification called STG (*Specialità Tradizionale Garantita*), which refers to the special characteristics of a particular dish, but there are no such products in Emilia Romagna. Yet.

For wines, the classification can be DOCG (*Denominazione di Origine Controllata e Garantita*), DOC (*Denominazione di Origine Controllata*), or IGT (*Indicazione Geografica Tipica*). A bottle of Chianti wine, for example, can either be a DOCG, DOC, or an IGT product, depending on the grapes used, the production process, and the certification.

In Emilia Romagna, this food classification system is taken very seriously. In fact, there are over 40 DOP and IGP products in Emilia Romagna—more than any other region in Italy, and even, the world. There aren't many other countries that focus as much on the certification of quality food products as Italy. The history of and pride in food is apparent when you walk through a food market in Emilia Romagna, or read a menu at a restaurant. The DOP and IGP system is how Emilia Romagna producers ensure the quality of traditional food products, and it is one of the reasons why food in Emilia Romagna is so good.

In many Northern European cities, like London or Amsterdam, if someone invites you over for dinner it is rude to talk about food. If you talk about a meal you have eaten prior, it would be considered rude to the host. Instead, you should talk only about the meal you are currently eating.

This concept does not exist in Emilia Romagna.

While touring Emilia Romagna, almost all conversations revolve around food and wine. About meals both past and present. At each meal, the conversation inevitably turns to what people are eating for dinner that night, or for lunch over the weekend. It's a constant and consistent theme.

One night, we walked into a bar in Modena for our predictable Aperol Spritz aperitivo. It was a typical bar, more functional than fancy. Large espresso machines, a few pastries and sandwiches on display. Cigarettes for sale.

We found the bartender and a customer watching a YouTube video on a laptop set on the counter. In fact, it was a bit difficult to even get their attention, they were so focused.

I peered over their shoulder and noticed what they were watching. It was a video about cooking an egg in a unique way. It was short, only a minute long. They watched this video over and over and over. If we had walked into a sports bar in the US and two men started analyzing an egg cooking video, they would probably be picked on, or worse, beat up.

How do Products Qualify as DOP or IGP?

The European Parliament provides the legal framework that will define the quality criteria for DOP and IGP products across the continent. These rules and regulations are the ones that producers, farmers, and breeders must follow in order to receive the mark of quality. Not only do the rules ensure quality, they also protect producers from competition from companies that produce fake products, ensuring consumers receive what they pay for.

When looking at the requirements for DOP and IGP products, all of the ingredients used to make the product must come from a particular region, or a designated area that is set forth in the guidelines. Strict rules must be followed to ensure quality production processes are used. (Some of these rules differ even within the region.)

The products, such as *Prosciutto di Parma,* will have a different set of guidelines than *Prosciutto di Modena*—even if, to the untrained eye, there's no difference. On a restaurant menu, it's possible to see prosciutto, but, it might not be official DOP Prosciutto di Parma. Unless it specifically says Prosciutto di Parma DOP, the meat's origins cannot be guaranteed.

As for the distinction between DOP and IGP certifications: DOP is the higher of the two standards, where IGP is a registered mark that signifies at least one phase of the production process is certified, or one important ingredient is from the local region. For example, there is an IGP certification for mortadella, which must be produced in a particular way. However, the pigs used need not be local, as would be required for a DOP certification—such as that for Prosciutto di Parma.

DOP certification is a lot more difficult to obtain. To be certified a DOP product, the ingredients must come from a particular territory, normally the most local. And, all production processes must also occur within the local area. The result is that, generally, DOP products are more expensive than IGP products, as there are literally no substitutions allowed.

Within Emilia Romagna, and throughout Europe, each of the DOP and IGP products is protected by a consortium responsible for maintaining the quality and providing certification. The European Union regulates these consortia, and producers must be members of the consortia in order to receive DOP or IGP designation.

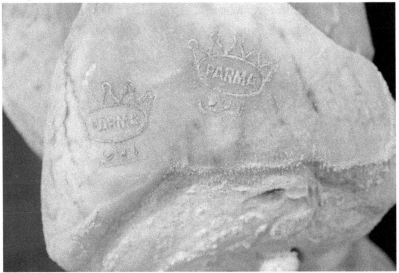

What are the DOP and IGP Products in Emilia Romagna?

Of the more than 40 DOP and IGP products certified in Emilia Romagna, a few stand out. These are the products that are most important to taste while traveling in Emilia Romagna. If possible, it's also a good idea to learn about how they are produced.

One of the most interesting of the 40 DOP and IGP products in Emilia Romagna is Mortadella Bologna. This is in great part because of its reputation overseas, particularly in the United States where it is more commonly known as bologna. In Emilia Romagna, there are specific rules on which cuts of meat can be used to make mortadella, which is an IGP product. For example: mortadella is usually made from the flank of the pig. The white bits inside are *not* bits of fat; rather, they're bits of pig cheek or pig neck, some of the most flavorful and tender cuts of meat.

Mortadella is just one of the many products that are guaranteed to be locally sourced. There is *Salame Cremona, Salami Piacentino,* and *Salame Felino* (yes, there are three different kinds of salami!) There is also *culatello*, which comes from the inside of the thigh of a pig and is aged in a very humid atmosphere to affect the flavor. *Pancetta di Piacenza* is another specialty cured meat, and a DOP product. *Zampone*, a special pig's trotter, is IGP.

There is, of course, balsamic vinegar from Modena, but also balsamic vinegar from Reggio Emilia. The rules and regulations for what is balsamic vinegar are staggering, as are the rules for how to properly taste balsamic vinegar. There is Parmigiano Reggiano and *Grana Padano*, two cheeses each with their own requirements and both receiving the DOP designation. There are two different kinds of DOP olive oil too.

But, Emilia Romagna is not just about balsamic vinegar, meats, and cheeses. Other, more surprising DOP and IGP products include chestnuts, asparagus, nectarines, pears, mushrooms, and even a kind of bread called *Coppia Ferrarese*. And newer designations are occurring all the time, including sour cherries, potatoes, onions, and even rice. With so many varied products being produced in just one region, you start to get the picture on how complex this culinary excursion can be.

A discussion of the DOP and IGP products from Emilia Romagna can be entirely overwhelming. In order to fully understand these products and their certification, you should tour the region to get a closer look at its different types of meats, cheeses, oils, and vinegars—not a bad way to spend a few weeks. (And we haven't even talked about pasta yet.)

As a side note: Italian products are marked with DOP and IGP. If their labels are written in English, however, look instead for PDO (Protected Designation of Origin) and PGI (Protected Geographical Indication). The PDO or PGI labels may be used by distributors outside of Italy, or can be used on English versions of menus within Italy.

2

CHEESE

Emilia Romagna is considered mecca by many cheese lovers. If you love cheese, and parmesan in particular, this is the place for you. There are about half a dozen DOP and IGP cheeses, and even more varieties that aren't certified, but are equally delicious.

Parmigiano Reggiano DOP – The King of Cheese

Parmigiano Reggiano is a DOP product and nothing like the generic parmesan found in supermarkets in the United States. Because of its DOP classification, cheese makers in Italy must follow specific rules to certify the cheese as Parmigiano Reggiano, rather than just regular old parmesan. The official Parmigiano Reggiano Cheese Consortium establishes these guidelines, and ensures that certified cheese makers follow them to a "T."

The consortium's rules and regulations cover not only the proper feeding of the dairy cows, but they also maintain an approved list of producers who can provide the feed. The rules also cover production standards, and regulations for fire branding the Parmigiano Reggiano mark.

In order to be deemed DOP Parmigiano Reggiano, the cheese can only be produced in the provinces of Parma, Reggio Emilia, Modena, or Bologna. There are over 350 dairies certified by the consortium as well as more than 3,500 cow breeders who can provide the milk. In total, approximately 50,000 employees work together in the production of Parmigiano Reggiano.

The process used to make Parmigiano Reggiano creates a cheese different from a lot of others, to the point that even lactose-intolerant people can eat it. It is so good, and so special, it rightfully deserves the name "The King of Cheese."

How They Make And Age Parmigiano Reggiano

The DOP regulations start with the cow. The milk used must come from a particular cow, raised in a particular area, and fed particular foods. The cows can only eat fresh or dry fodder, and are not allowed to eat any fermented products or animal derivatives. This ensures that the milk they produce is of a very high quality even before the production begins. The color of the cheese itself proves that the cattle were fed only fresh fodder. This color can also change throughout the year depending on the season, and the color of the food the cows have eaten.

The DOP Consortium lays down the law that only three ingredients are allowed in the production of Parmigiano Reggiano: milk, rennet, and salt. Rennet is an enzyme that comes from the cow itself and, together with the whey starter used from the previous day's production, aids in the curdling process.

The production process is also regulated by the consortium. Evening milk is skimmed and mixed with fresh, whole, morning milk. Then, it's heated in large copper cauldrons. After the rennet is added, it takes about 20 minutes for the milk to form curds.

The curds are then broken up using a giant whisk. The mixture is heated to a specific temperature for a set amount of time, after which the cheese makers carefully prepare the large mass of cheese to be removed from the cauldron, still steaming from the heat. The large mass of cheese is so big it takes two men to help form the cheese and move it from the cauldron.

Once the cheese forms a solid mass, it's then cut into two parts and wrapped in a traditional cloth. The process of moving the cheese is a well-choreographed dance between two Italian men. The process is also painstakingly precise, giving way to the nickname *parmigiano bambino*, or parmigiano baby, as the cheese is wrapped and unwrapped, and wrapped again in its comfy little blanket. The cheese is then placed into a mold to give it the signature wheel shape.

After the cheese settles, it's given a unique number, which becomes the wheel's identity card, along with a branding that states the month and year of production. A few days later, the enormous cheese wheel is immersed in a water and salt solution. The cheese wheel absorbs the salt, acting as a preservative.

In order to age the cheese, the wheels are set out in long rows in an aging room. A dream come true for cheese lovers is to stand in a room filled wall to wall, floor to ceiling, with giant wheels of cheese. Once you step into the aging room, a strong cheese smell will fill your nose. It is an intoxicating mix of sharp and pungent odors. This experience alone is worth a trip to Emilia Romagna!

The cheese wheel receives its DOP branding after aging for 12 months. In order to be considered Parmigiano Reggiano DOP, though, the cheese must age an additional six months. Thus, the minimum amount of time the cheese is aged (according to DOP rules) is 18 months.

In order to further improve the flavor, some *caseifici*, or creameries, age their cheeses even longer; some up to 60 months or more. Do the math. Yeah, that's cheese aged in a special room for five years! As the cheese ages it becomes a little more chalky and crumbly, and some say a lot more delicious. The outside of the cheese dries without the addition of any additives, which is why it's also possible to eat the rind of a good Parmigiano Reggiano. Nothing goes to waste.

In order to be fire-branded with the official Parmigiano Reggiano logo, each and every wheel must be inspected and approved by the DOP Consortium. The cheese inspector uses a hammer, screw-needle, and sampling dowel. With this hammer, the inspector taps the cheese at various points while listening carefully to the way the crust responds to the hammer.

The cheese wheel is then pierced with the screw-needle to extract a small sample of the contents. The cheese inspector uses this sample to test the smell, taste, and age of the cheese. The sampling dowel is used when the hammer and screw-needle don't result in a proper inspection. If the wheel of cheese satisfies the inspector, it is fire-branded with the distinctive Parmigiano Reggiano logo, and marked DOP. Cheese that does not pass inspection can still be sold, but it will not be certified DOP.

In the end, approximately 550 liters (or over 145 gallons) of milk are needed to produce one wheel of Parmigiano Reggiano, which will weigh approximately 40 kilograms (or almost 90 pounds). Over three million wheels of cheese are produced each year, each one distinctively marked with the characteristic pin dot writing that provides the code of the dairy, the month and year of production, and the famous Parmigiano Reggiano fire mark. These are all seals of good quality and, of course, great taste.

Grana Padano DOP

If Parmigiano Reggiano is the King of Cheese, perhaps Grana Padano could be considered the Queen of Cheese. Often confused with Parmigiano Reggiano, Grana Padano has its own characteristics that make it unique.

Grana Padano is produced in several areas in the north of Italy, most of which lie outside of Emilia Romagna—such as Trento and Padua. But within Emilia Romagna, Piacenza produces a DOP Grana Padano, which has been famous since the 16th century. The Conzorio Tutela Grana Padano establishes similar rules to the consortium that regulates Parmigiano Reggiano.

At first glance, many people might get Parmigiano Reggiano and Grana Padano confused. Whereas Parmigiano Reggiano is produced using only three ingredients (milk, salt, and rennet), Grana Padano also includes an enzyme. Parmigiano Reggiano cows are fed only dry fodder, whereas Grana Padano cows can be fed fermented fodder. The addition of the enzyme is required because the cows are eating fermented fodder.

To make Parmigiano Reggiano, skimmed and whole milk are mixed together, but for Grana Padano, only skimmed milk is used. Parmigiano Reggiano can only be made once a day, whereas Grana Padano can be made twice a day. The minimum amount of aging required for Grana Padano is only nine months, instead of the 18 required for Parmigiano Reggiano.

Grana Padano is generally cheaper than Parmigiano Reggiano. The cost relates to how many areas produce each type of cheese, how much land is available for grazing, and what the cows are fed. As a result of these factors, more Grana Padano is produced each year than Parmigiano Reggiano. Because Grana Padano is a little less nutty, and a bit more subtle in flavor, it is often used in many dishes where Parmigiano Reggiano would be too harsh a flavor.

Our formaggio di fossa experience was like something you'd watch Anthony Bourdain talk about, or even better, Andrew Zimmern, because as far as cheese goes, this certainly qualifies as a "Bizarre Food."

After a long morning tasting Italian wines with Helena from Yummy Italy, we started making our way to the village of Sogliano, high in the hills of Romagna. We were southeast of Bologna, and northeast of Florence, almost to Rimini and the Adriatic Sea. A part of Italy we've never visited before.

Earlier in the day it was hot and humid, with blue cloudless skies. By the time we reached the hill top village of Sogliano al Rubicone, grey skies had overtaken Emilia Romagna. A mist had set over the hills, making the entire experience seem a little, well, eerie.

We climbed the hillside in Helena's car, in the grey and mist, to see a man about a cave filled with cheese. This is what I love about traveling in Emilia Romagna. I never before would have assumed those words would cross my lips.

Formaggio di Fossa DOP – Cave Cheese

You can be pretty sure that only true cheese aficionados travel to Emilia Romagna to learn about *formaggio di fossa*, or "cave cheese." How many people outside Italy have even heard of cave cheese?

The history of cave cheese dates back to the Middle Ages, when people of the region began hiding food in large holes in the ground in order to protect their food supply from invaders. The word *fossa* translates to pit, although cave cheese seems to be a more popular interpretation.

Formaggio di fossa is produced in several areas but is probably most often associated with Sogliano al Rubbicone. The Formaggio di Fossa di Sogliano DOP is produced under strict regulations. Simply put, it is pecorino sheep's milk cheese that is aged inside a pit in the ground. The DOP regulations focus not only on how the cheese is made, but also how it's aged. It's a more unique aging process than the process for producing Parmigiano Reggiano.

For the DOP version of Formaggio di Fossa di Sogliano, cheesemakers produce wheels of cheese and prepare them for aging. Farmers and people from around the village (and sometimes from all over Italy) will also produce their own wheels of cheese. They will bring their cheese to the owners of the pit. Each wheel that is set to be submerged is wrapped in a cloth bag, and tagged or marked. The cheese wheels are also weighed before they're placed in the pit. Although all of the cheese is aged in the pit, only those that are produced and controlled by the cheese makers themselves are eligible to receive the DOP classification—though everyone else is rewarded with tasty cheese.

The pits are up to 16 feet deep and lined with straw, which creates a cool but humid space for aging cheese. The straw is burned in the days before the pit is filled to sterilize the space, then more straw is added, along with scaffolding to maintain the structure of the pit.

The pit is opened and filled in August. Over a two week period, farmers and villagers arrive at the cheese ager, to deposit their wheels of cheese. The wheels are lowered into the pit, piled one on top of another. The pit is covered with a piece of wood, then sand, and finally a plaster-like substance, which seals the pit entirely.

The wheels are left for about three months in the pits. During this time an anaerobic fermentation process occurs due to the lack of oxygen. Gravity takes over as the weight of one wheel on top of another presses all of the cheese together. The fat drips down through the cheese wheels and out the bottom. This also reduces the size of each wheel. This fermentation process gives the cheese a particular smell and taste, which is what makes cave cheese so unique.

The cheese is always revealed on Saint Catherine's Day in November. When the cave is opened, a noxious odor escapes the pit. It can be so strong that people have actually died from the fumes!

At this point the cheese becomes formaggio di fossa, or cave cheese. Villagers pick up their cheese and pay for the aging process based on how much the cheese weighs at the end of the process.

When the cave cheese emerges, it is entirely different from the softer cheese that was placed in the pit three months before. It is firm or semi-firm; the color is more yellow and, most notably, it's pungent in both smell and taste.

Something also occurs during the fermentation process that makes the cave cheese easier to digest by people who are lactose intolerant. So that's good news. Eat Formaggio di Fossa di Sogliano on its own or with seasonal preserves or honey. It can also be drizzled with traditional balsamic vinegar.

In addition to eating cave cheese on its own, it's used in a lot of regional recipes. It can be sprinkled over pasta for flavoring, including one of the most unique pastas in Emilia Romagna: *passatelli*.

The Soft Cheeses

In Emilia Romagna, there are two soft cheeses, one of which is very well known. The other? Not so much.

Ricotta

Ricotta cheese is known around the world as the perfect ingredient to stuff ravioli or layer in a lasagna. It's a fresh, mild cheese, sometimes with large curds that make it look more like cottage cheese.

Ricotta is made throughout Italy, wherever cheese is produced. In Emilia Romagna, most Parmigiano Reggiano producers also make ricotta from the byproduct of their main cheese production. Ricotta is made from whey, the liquid that remains after the Parmigiano Reggiano is made. After fermentation, the ricotta (literally meaning "recooked" in Italian), is cooked again, until it almost boils. Afterwards, it solidifies until curds are formed and then it is filtered through a cloth. Each morning, it's possible to see at least one person on the edge of the Parmigiano Reggiano production, standing over steaming buckets of fresh ricotta cheese.

Ricotta is not a DOP product within Emilia Romagna. Confusion may arise, however, with one of the most famous ricotta cheeses, Ricotta Romana DOP. This DOP product is from Lazio, the region where Rome is located. It is *Romana*, not *Romagna*. It's a one letter difference, but a big difference in Italy.

There are many types of pastas filled with ricotta in Emilia Romagna, but one of the most unique ways to enjoy ricotta is to enjoy it smothered in a sweet syrup called *saba*. Saba is made from the same grapes that are used to make balsamic vinegar, but it's a lot sweeter and more concentrated. That just means it is even more tasty on a scoop of ricotta.

Ricotta

Squacquerone DOP

Now, what about that cheese most people don't know about? It's the one with a funny sounding name: *squacquerone*, a DOP cheese from Romagna, produced at the edge of Emilia Romagna, along the Adriatic Sea.

Similar to ricotta, Squacquerone DOP is made from cow's milk that's been curdled. Pasteurized milk is heated, liquid rennet is added, and the cheese quickly curdles, generally in less than 30 minutes. The excess liquid is drained as it stands. The cheese is placed in a mold, in hot and humid rooms, then placed in a salted brine. After the cheese obtains the right consistency, it matures in a cold fridge for a few days.

There is no aging process. Instead, squacquerone is always eaten fresh, generally within three days. Squacquerone is most often served with a typical bread from Romagna, *piadina*. The chilled fresh cheese is spread on a hot piadina, where it starts to melt until creamy, and topped with arugula.

Squacquerone does not have a rind, and is as soft as cheeses come, often looking wobbly as it arrives at the table. It's slightly watery, resulting in the "aqua" portion of its name. There is an acidic taste to it and it pairs nicely with fruit preserves and balsamic vinegar. Plus, it's just fun to say.

Tracking Down a Cheese Maker in Italy

To understand the process of how they make Parmigiano Reggiano and other cheeses, go behind the scenes to observe a cheese maker in Italy producing his masterpiece. The parmigiano making process is fascinating and you can learn more about it in the hills outside of Modena.

After a tour, be sure to purchase some parmigiano to support the caseficio. But be careful, even the smallest piece is a sizable chunk of cheese that will last you a good while, even if you're cheese-obsessed. Most producers offer vacuum sealed cheese as well, for easy transport home.

Recommended Casefici

All production of Parmigiano Reggiano takes place in the morning, and usually finishes around 11 am. This is because they use the milk that was collected the evening before. Plan your visit to a caseficio in the morning to have the best chance of seeing the cheese makers at work. It's usually possible to see ricotta being made at the same caseficio during your tour.

Caseficio 4 Madonne

One of the more commercial makers of Parmigiano Reggiano, is also one of the easiest to visit. Caseificio 4 Madonne is a *cooperativa*, or collection, of cheese producers. Different dairies from the region deliver their milk, twice a day, to the caseficio. At its modern and recently renovated facilities, the tour takes you through the different stages of the production process and ends in the aging room where you'll be surrounded by over 30,000 wheels of cheese. Guided tours are offered every day but require bookings via their website at least one week ahead of time.

Caseficio 4 Madonne, Strada Lesignana, 130, 41123, Lesignana (MO). Located only ten minutes outside of Modena city center.

(http://www.caseificio4madonne.it/en/)

Museum of Parmigiano Reggiano

In the town of Soragna, in the province of Parma, lies an entire museum dedicated to the history and production of Parmigiano Reggiano. Part of Parma's Museo dei Cibo, or "Museums of Food," it stands in a restored castle, where cheese was once produced. On display are artifacts that have been used to produce Parmigiano Reggiano in five areas of Emilia Romagna.

(www.museidelcibo.it)

Parmigiano Reggiano Museum, Corte Castellazzi, Via Volta 5, Soragna (PR). Open from March 1 to December 8 on the weekends between 10:00 am and 1:00 pm, and 3:00 pm to 6:00 pm. Tours are also available on weekdays by appointment only. A visit to the museum is €5 and includes a tasting.

(http://www.parmigianoreggiano.com/)

Artisanal Producers and Cooperativa

It's also possible to visit smaller producers of Parmigiano Reggiano. Often times the cheese shops are open for tasting and shopping, but it is a bit harder to see the cheese makers at work. Most of these operations are limited to four or five employees, often family members, so tours are difficult to offer, and language can be a barrier. To book a visit to a smaller producer, it's better to work with a local culinary tour operator, though you can send the producers an email and see what happens.

Caseificio Montardone, Via Giardini Nord, 7087, Serramazzoni (MO).

(http://www.caseificio-montardone.it/contatti/)

Caseificio Nuova Martignana, Via Martiniana, 281, 41126, Baggiovara (MO)

(http://www.caseificionuovamartignana.it/index)

Formaggio di Fossa

The village of Sogliano al Rubicone, in the hills of Romagna, is a village with several cave cheese producers. It's possible to stop by shops in Sogliano to purchase cave cheese, but most of the shops either do not run tours and tastings, or they don't speak English.

Fossa Pellegrini operates a shop and runs a small cave cheese museum behind their house. They are a small operation, run by a husband and wife. In this case, it is better to book the experience through a culinary tour operator to learn more about the production process. If you are a true foodie, you won't regret it.

Perhaps the easiest way to taste formaggio di fossa is to look for dishes on menus that say *con formaggio di fossa*. Be prepared for the sharp taste.

3

MEAT

New travelers to Italy, or even to Spain, may look at the cured meats of those countries with trepidation. For many, particularly travelers who grew up in the United States, any meat that came encased was a hot dog. If it was sliced from a deli counter, it was processed lunch meat. Maybe it was liverwurst. Or olive loaf. Fake turkey meat. Processed boiled ham. This is not American dining at its best, and is hardly related to the cured meats available in Europe.

When you start delving into Italian cured meats, it quickly becomes clear there is more to it than merely processed meats. To some, prosciutto may seem pink and raw, pancetta fatty, and mortadella, well, baloney. It is round and pink, and "processed." But, this could not be further from the truth.

In Emilia Romagna, plates of sliced, cured meat, or *salumi*, are a staple of eating; maybe even more so than in other parts of Italy. The following list only includes a handful of products, the ones a traveler is most likely to come across in Emilia Romagna.

Mortadella Bologna IGP

Many kids who grew up in the U.S. grew up on bologna sandwiches. Think round plastic containers, with a yellow backing. Think of the sound made when your mom ripped open the packaging. If you were truly *lucky*, perhaps you remember the smell of the bologna when it sizzled in a pan, in preparation for a fried bologna sandwich—an "all American lunch" served to kids across the country.

For travelers to Emilia Romagna, it's understandable to confuse mortadella with its counterpart in the United States: bologna. It's not clear how the mortadella that was eaten by Italian-American immigrants turned into American bologna. Obviously, there's the connection that mortadella was from Bologna. What's not clear is what bologna became considering its grandfather is a meat that has been known for its high quality for centuries.

There has always been the running joke that no one knows what kind of meat is really in bologna. This is the first thing that differs from its Italian grandfather. Mortadella is made from 100% pork meat. Mortadella is one of the many DOP and IGP products in

Italy, meaning its production is strictly regulated for quality. You certainly can't say the same about bologna.

According to Dictionary.com:

> *The bologna sausage is traditionally made from the "odds and ends" of chicken, turkey, beef, or pork. It is similar to the Italian mortadella, which originated in the Italian city of Bologna. The inexpensive deli meat is often pronounced and spelled "baloney."*

Granted this little nugget came from dictionary.com and should not be quoted as a certifiable reference on the history of food. But it highlights the discrepancy that exists over the term mortadella, aka bologna sausage, aka baloney.

So, how is real mortadella made? It's a fairly simple process that involves a few different steps of pressing and grinding pork meat, along with the characteristic white bits of "fat." Those white bits are actually the meat from the throat or cheek of the pig. In a high quality mortadella, the white bits should remain connected to the pink meat after it is cut. If the white pieces start to separate, you are definitely not eating a high quality mortadella.

Essentially, all of the meat is mixed with a little seasoning, including salt and white pepper. The pressed meat is squeezed into a giant casing. The casing is tied at one end, and then the entire mortadella (which weights at least 12 kilograms, or about 25 pounds) is carefully tied over and over again. There is an art to the tying process, as a producer turns the large mortadella around, multiple times, while crisscrossing the white string to tie the giant piece of meat together.

The tying helps the mortadella retain its shape while it hangs and while it's cooked in a large, dry oven for about 22 hours. Before cooking, the raw mortadella is a pale pink, but afterwards the exterior turns a deep rosy red.

That dictionary.com definition is still mystifying, as is the link between mortadella from Bologna and bologna from America—where it's made from "odds and ends." Mortadella is made with high quality pork and virtually nothing else, so when you see it on a menu in Emilia Romagna, please don't dismiss it based solely on its American namesake.

As we started to travel throughout Italy, and we became budding connoisseurs of Italian food, I started to grow accustomed to Italian cured meats. I now crave them, and am usually the one to suggest ordering a giant plate of meat, and am usually left licking my fingers at the end of the course.

When one of these platters of meat is delivered to our table and I see thinly sliced pieces of mortadella, I get almost giddy. I want to pick the slice up above my face, lift my chin, and allow the sliced mortadella to descend into my open mouth. I imagine that I look a little like a seal excited to be fed a big fish. But, I don't care, because I love a good mortadella.

Just don't call it baloney.

Mortadella is an IGP product, and the Mortadella Bologna

Consortium controls the quality of all producers, ensuring they adhere to the traditional recipe. Interestingly, the consortium promotes the nutritional values of mortadella: a full pound of mortadella has about 288 calories—less than a plate of pasta. And, it is low in cholesterol. When ordering mortadella in Bologna, look for the snail logo associated with the Slow Food Presidium. The snail logo indicates it is a truly artisan product, and not mass produced.

The mortadella in Emilia Romagna is either sliced thin or cubed. Many prefer the thinly sliced mortadella, which tastes smooth and fresh, and is light years away from the bologna you might have tried in the U.S. Italians would never consider frying up mortadella and throwing it on a piece of bread with some ketchup. In fact, after enjoying mortadella in Emilia Romagna, you probably couldn't imagine eating a fried bologna sandwich ever again.

Prosciutto di Parma

Walk around any small town in Italy and you're bound to come across a handful of shops with cured meat in the window. Walk in and look up. Chances are that large legs of ham will be hanging from the ceiling. More often than not, they will be stamped with a crown shaped marking that bears a single word: "Parma."

Prosciutto di Parma, or more generally, Parma ham, has been around since Roman times. There are stories from 100 B.C. referencing the unique flavor of the air-dried pork from the area surrounding Parma. At the time, pork was dried to extend its life and prevent it from spoiling.

A group of Parma ham producers created a Consortium, *Consorzio del Prosciutto di Parma*, in the seventies, to control the quality of prosciutto. In 1996, the European Union conferred the DOP designation on Prosciutto di Parma. It was one of the first meats to be awarded the status. A leg of ham can only be considered Prosciutto di Parma DOP if it meets the strict guidelines of the Consortium.

Similar to other DOP products, the production of Parma ham is highly regulated and limited solely to the area surrounding Parma. Unlike other meats, such as culatello or pancetta, where pigs must come from the immediate vicinity, the Parma ham pigs can be raised within 10 regions around Italy. It's still local, but not local to the extreme.

The pigs' diet is regulated too. The special breeds must only be fed a blend of grains, cereals, and whey from Parmigiano Reggiano. (Yes, the pigs are fattened on the King of Cheese!) This ensures that the taste and smell of the prosciutto is consistent. The pigs must be at least nine months old and weigh a minimum of 140 kilograms (a little over 300 pounds) in order to be used in the production of a DOP Prosciutto.

The Consortium likes to say there are only four ingredients in Parma ham: Italian pigs, salt, air, and time. In reality it's really only two ingredients, although air and time are also key components. Unlike mortadella, where a variety of seasonings are used, Parma ham is made by curing a leg of pork with nothing but sea salt. This increases the tenderness of the meat, and gives it a characteristic sweet flavor.

The production process is intense and easy to witness when traveling to Emilia Romagna. It's overseen by a *maestro salatore*, or salt master, which has to be the coolest sounding title for a ham maker.

After receiving the hind legs of the pig, they are thoroughly covered, and to some extent massaged, with massive amounts of sea salt. The leg of ham is placed lying down, inside giant refrigerators, allowing the meat to cold-dry for about a week. After it is removed and a second layer of salt is added, the ham continues to dry cold for another 15 to 18 days. The ham is moved from room to room, being alternately washed and cleaned, and hung in refrigerated rooms or drying rooms.

Over the next three months, the hams are hung in large, well ventilated rooms. Similar to the Parmigiano Reggiano aging rooms, the smell is intoxicating. Often, they are hung in rows a half a dozen hams high, and dozens of hams long. Legs of ham as far as the eye can see.

The unique thing about the drying rooms are the large windows that are opened when the outside temperature and humidity levels are just right. This allows the ham to be exposed to the climate of Parma, and the air: the fourth "ingredient" in Parma ham.

During this time, the meat starts to change color. Whereas initially the hams are bright pink, soft, and tender, the meat darkens, dries, and ultimately is hardened. The exposed surfaces of the ham, though, are periodically softened with a lard and salt substance, called *sugna*, to control the drying process. The goal is to allow the ham to dry, but not too quickly. By the end of the process, it's not uncommon for a ham to have lost about a quarter of its weight solely because of the loss of moisture.

After seven months of drying, salting, curing, and massaging, the ham is transferred to an aging room, or cellar. This is where the curing process is completed. The Consortium dictates that Parma ham must be cured at least one year, which is timed from the date of the first salting—although it's possible to have Prosciutto di Parma aged for as long as three years or more.

When ready, an inspector from the Consortium arrives to test each and every leg of ham. The inspector pierces the leg at five specific points with a thin horse bone needle, smelling the bone after each time it is removed from the ham. By smelling the meat, with a highly trained nose, it's possible to confirm the quality of the ham. It is only after the leg passes inspection, and is fire branded with the signature five point crown, that the ham officially becomes Prosciutto di Parma.

Only 160 producers in all of Italy are certified by the Consortium to produce Parma ham. (That may seem like a lot, particularly in comparison to meats such as culatello.) But, considering the pure volume of prosciutto consumed around the world, it is nothing short of a miracle. The Consortium certifies between eight- and nine-million legs of Parma ham each year.

There is Prosciutto di Parma, and there is prosciutto. It's possible to see prosciutto on a restaurant menu without it being certified by the Parma Consortium. It might be made in Parma, but not from the right kind of pigs. It might be made in a similar process, but made elsewhere. It might be filled with nitrates, rather than being all natural. Essentially, prosciutto translates to "dried out," and can be used to describe any dried pork. It's important to know what kind of prosciutto is on the menu.

Or it could be Prosciutto di Modena DOP, its neighbor to the east. To a layman it would be hard to tell the difference between the two types of DOP prosciutto. They each have a consortium (Modena's is actually older) that protects quality. They each come from Italian raised pigs. They are each salted and cured, but Prosciutto di Modena must be aged at least 14 months, not 12, as in Parma. The Prosciutto di Modena is also fire branded, with a large P and a small m, in place of the Prosciutto di Parma crown.

Or, it could be Prosciutto di San Daniele. But that's not in Emilia Romagna, so it is a ham story for another day. There are several other DOP prosciutto products from all over Italy. Regardless of whether the prosciutto you eat while traveling in Emilia

Romagna is *di Parma* or *di Modena* or *di* somewhere else, it's bound to be tasty!

Culatello di Zibello

Culatello is often referred to as the King of Salumi. After learning about the production process, and the cost, it's clear why.

Although there are references to culatello dating back to wedding feasts in the 1300s, its verifiable history started around 1735 near Parma. Culatello was also discussed in poetry from the 19th century. (Isn't that so Italian? References to a cured meat in an Italian poem referencing the peasant culture.)

The Roman army usually established their winter encampments in Parma. It's possible they started to salt their meat there to have it ready for their summer military campaigns as salt was readily available from the thermal waters of Salsomaggiore.

Although culatello has been produced for centuries in Emilia Romagna, only recently has it received some notoriety outside of Italy. Historically, culatello has been overshadowed by prosciutto. The culatello regulations are more strict, and it is therefore harder to produce than prosciutto. This makes culatello more rare. Demand outstrips supply and therefore culatello is more expensive. There is also something just a little bit different about culatello. Culatello's unique characteristics result from the aging process.

Culatello is a more recently named DOP product, with its Consortium in operation for less than ten years. There are only 21 producers licensed to make culatello, in less than ten locations along the Po River. Although the Po River runs across almost the entire span of Northern Italy, the portion of the Po where culatello is produced is only a small stretch of the river.

The Consortium's goal is to not only ensure quality, but also that the producers respect traditions and age the culatello using what might be considered old-fashioned methods. For example, culatello must be handmade.

Culatello, the most well known of which is Culatello di Zibello DOP, has a signature pear shape. Using the muscular inner thigh of the pig, it is made by wrapping the deboned meat in a natural pork bladder. (The same cut of meat is used for prosciutto, but for culatello, producers trim the meat more, and remove the bone.) The meat is salted with black pepper, and sometimes garlic. Some producers also use a dry white wine to help season and preserve the meat. Only pigs both born and raised in Emilia Romagna, or in nearby Lombardy, may be used.

Thus far, there is no significant difference in the production of culatello, in comparison to salumi. The distinctive flavor, however, comes from the aging process. Similar to the aging of Prosciutto di Modena, which was aged outdoors in generations past, culatello is produced in the flatlands along the Po River. It's aged a minimum of ten months in a cave or a *cantina*. The exposure to the climate is what provides culatello with its unique flavor.

When learning about culatello, fog always seems to come into play. The area along the Po River, including Zibello, has long, cold, and foggy winters. Summers are sunny and hot. The vast differential between the cold and hot weather, of the humidity and the dryness, provides the distinctive flavor and fragrance characteristic of culatello. Culatello might be thought of as similar to prosciutto, but it is darker, stronger in flavor, and drier. And, because of its rarity outside of Italy, it is a must-eat in Emilia Romagna.

Pancetta Piacentina DOP

Pancetta is the fatty member of the Italian cured meats. But, fat is flavor. Its characteristic ribbons of alternating red and white certainly add color to any platter of cured meats. It's much softer than other cured meats—even prosciutto. For fat lovers, it can simply melt in your mouth or be eaten on a warm piece of bread. There is almost an art to slicing pancetta, which must be cut very thin to ensure that melt-in-the-mouth deliciousness.

Similar to culatello, pancetta is only produced from pigs that are born and bred in Emilia Romagna or Lombardy. The production process itself only occurs within the province of Piacenza, at the western edge of Emilia Romagna. Like other Italian cured meats, it is said that the distinctive flavor is due the local climate within the region. Pancetta is one of three DOP meats produced in Piacenza, with coppa and Salame Piacentino being the other two. Piacenza is actually the only province in the EU to have three DOP salami products.

For Pancetta Piacentina DOP, producers use the central part of the pig, including the pork belly and back fat. Even large scale producers of pancetta still must be bound by traditional production methods. First, the meat is dry salted with a mix of salt and spices, sometimes including cloves. The meats are left to cold-dry, similar to prosciutto. Then it's massaged, rolled, and bound to give the pancetta its distinctive shape. They are dried for about 10-15 days, then matured for at least three months. Each pancetta will weigh between five and eight kilograms.

Other IGP and DOP Meats

There is more to the Italian meats of Emilia Romagna than mortadella, prosciutto, culatello, and pancetta—though those are, probably, the most important ones for a food lover to track down. There are a few other meats, however, with an IGP or DOP designation that may be found on restaurant menus in the region.

Coppa

Coppa is a pork-neck salami, and not to be confused with *coppa di testa*, which is head cheese. There are two types of *coppa* found in Emilia Romagna: Coppa Piacentina DOP, from Piacenza (as the name suggests), and Coppa di Parma IGP. Traditionally, coppa was served by families during the holidays or important events. The recipe would be passed down through generations.

Coppa is made with a round cut of pork that runs from where the shoulder and neck meet to the ribs. The pork is either stuffed into a cow or a pig intestine, and flavored with salt, pepper, and other seasonings, often including cinnamon. It can also be seasoned with wine. Coppa is aged between six months to a year. For Coppa Piacentina, it must be produced in the region, at an altitude less than 3,000 feet above sea level. Although the meat can come from Emilia Romagna or Lombardy, it must only be produced, and cured, within the territory of Piacenza.

The meat itself is in an oblong casing, with a marbled white and deep red color. On a plate it might look a little similar to Pancetta, but would be less soft, and less fatty. Similar to pancetta, there is also an art to slicing coppa, to ensure it is sufficiently thin.

Cotechino and Zampone

Two of the meats in Emilia Romagna that are probably least known to Americans, and probably many Europeans, are *Cotechino Modena IGP* and *Zampone Modena IGP*.

Cotechino is a fresh sausage, meaning it is not cured or aged. It is made with pork, back fat, and pork rinds. Traditionally, it was a way to serve the less tender cuts of meat. The meat is ground, placed inside a casing, boiled, and cooked in a dry oven. Afterwards, it is vacuum packed, making it one of the few meats in Emilia Romagna to be found in a box.

Zampone is similar to cotechino in that it is a fresh sausage, ground with salt, seasonings, and pork rinds. The difference is that the sausage is stuffed inside a pork trotter, or the foot and front leg of the pig. The pork meat can be a mixed bag including tasty pig cheek, but also head, throat, or shoulder meat. Because it takes so long to cook zampone, it is often pre-cooked and also sold vacuum packed, sometimes also in a box.

During the winter months, it's common to find both cotechino and zampone served with lentils or white beans, along with mashed potatoes. They are both hearty dishes, often reserved for Christmas or New Year. It's not as common to see them on restaurant menus in and around Modena. But when you do find them, you know it is a traditional restaurant. One notable location that serves cotechino is Ristorante Da Danilo in the center of Modena.

Salame and Salami

Salame refers to a singular round of cured meat; *salami*, is the plural of salame, in Italian. *Salumi* is a more generic term for cured meats, and generally cured pork products. When it comes to salami, Emilia Romagna knows what it's doing.

There are almost a half dozen versions of IGP and DOP salami produced across Emilia Romagna. Although it's possible to find these versions by name when at an Italian deli or *salumeria*, it's less likely that you can order specific versions of salami by name from a restaurant menu. They will normally be part of an antipasto meat platter, but it is possible to see individual cuts of salami on a menu.

Salame Piacentino DOP is made of lean pork meat, with very little fat. The flavor is made more intense by additional aging of the salame, which starts at a minimum of 45 days. Individual salame can weigh up to one kilogram. Similar to pancetta, the pork may come from either Lombardy or Emilia Romagna, but the production and ripening must only occur in the province of Piacenza. There are similar limits as well to its aging in lower altitudes.

You can also find Salame Cremona IGP on menus in Piacenza. Resulting from the processing of pork meat with salt and crushed garlic, the meat is aged for a minimum of five weeks, and can be aged up to four months. It is deep red in color and carries with it a little spice from the garlic. This version of salami has been produced in the Po Valley since Roman times. Although Cremona is technically just over the border in Lombardy, it's still a common salame product in Piacenza.

Artisanal Meat Production in Emilia Romagna

Many *agriturismi* and small restaurants in Emilia Romagna produce their own meats, particularly salami, on premise. One such place is Corte San Ruffillo, where Sara and Luca run a farm and winery, a contemporary Romagna restaurant, and a lovely hotel. Luca also makes his own salumi and ages them in a meat cellar.

The meat cellar is underneath the main part of the resort, an old stone manor house from the 14th century which has been restored lovingly. Sara and Luca live in an apartment on the first floor with their family. The meat cellar is just underneath. It's a small stone room, with arched ceilings; nothing like the prosciutto factories dotted throughout Parma and Modena.

Luca's meat production is artisanal. It's experimental. The main purpose of the production is to provide fabulous meats to the restaurant at Corte San Ruffillo. Curing meat is an ancient process across Europe: It started out of necessity, looking for a way to preserve meats to last through the winter.

Now, it is an art form.

Luca uses local pigs to make salami, culatello, and coppa. He cures pork belly, and uses pork cheek, or *guanciale*. He rubs the meats with salt, pepper, and sometimes even coffee. Each one is labeled with the Corte San Ruffillo brand on a metal tag.

Different kinds of mold form on the outside of the meats as they age, in shades of white, green, and pink. There are good types of mold, and not so good. The latter will make an inferior product. Many of the larger producers will actually control the production to ensure more consistency, which means there is less natural mold. They may brush flour on the final product solely for cosmetic purposes; to make salami look more like salami. Luca makes his products all-natural. In fact, he is limiting the use of flour on some of the meats to ensure they are gluten-free.

There are artisanal meat producers located all across the region. Winemakers, restaurants, and agriturismi will often produce their own cured meats. They may focus on using particular animal breeds, and limit their ingredients to make very high-quality, and interesting meats. These may be of great quality, and offer a fabulous alternative to DOP and IGP products. But unless they are certified by the local consortium, they would not be labeled as a DOP or IGP product. This does not mean producers like Luca are serving inferior products. It can be quite the opposite as Luca might be able to experiment more, to use different seasonings, or different production or aging methods that could, in fact, make an excellent product. This is to say, don't turn your nose down at a product only because it is not marked with a DOP or IGP designation.

When the owner of an Italian country resort asks if you want to tour their private meat cellar, what are you supposed to say? Of course you accept the offer.

The way Luca, of Corte San Ruffillo, looks at the meats hung in his meat cellar. The way he inspects the meats. The way he tenderly rubs the meats. His wife, Sara, points to him and says, "His babies," with a roll of the eyes that thousands of woman have used when describing their husbands' pursuits. I know I have.

I told Luca that if he returned to the meat cellar the following day and one of the salami was missing, it was because Eric tucked one into his jacket. When Eric jokingly threatened to sneak into the meat cellar at night, Sara was quick to remind us that they sleep right upstairs and would hear everything.

Instead, Eric would have to settle for eating the cured meats that they serve at the restaurant —an equally good plan, without the element of risk involved in an international meat heist.

The "Meat Breads" of Emilia Romagna

After learning about the history and production of Italian cured meats, it's necessary to taste them. This is the easiest part of learning about the meats of Emilia Romagna. Almost every restaurant, *trattoria*, or *osteria* offers a starter platter of cured meats, often served with a regional bread. It's almost as though there is an entire category of Italian bread that can be called "meat breads." The regional meat breads are amazing, and change across the region.

One of the most popular ways to eat cured meat is with *gnocco fritto*, a deep fried puff of bread popular in and around Modena. It is similar to *torta fritta*, which is popular around Parma. The bread is sliced open in order to pop a slice of mortadella inside. The best gnocco fritto is served warm, so the bread melts the meat just a bit. Meat heaven. It's also possible to find dessert versions of gnocco fritto, served with Nutella.

Another bread that is found on many menus in and around Modena is *tigelle*, or *crescentine*, a dense round bread almost like the cousin of an English muffin. Tigelle is made by rolling the dough into a round ball and then pressing it on a heavy cast iron, or aluminum style pan, called a *tigelliera*. Essentially, it's a mold, similar to a waffle iron, but placed directly on the stove, which makes about five to six at a time. The top is pulled down and the dough is pressed to form tigelle.

Traditionally, the bread molds were made of clay and placed in the fire, but now they are usually made on the stove top. (In commercial establishments, it is often just as likely the tigelle are made in electric versions, which can make up to eight at a time.) The molds normally have a decorative flower design on them, which is then pressed into each piece of bread.

When a basket of tigelle arrive at a table, they are always warm. Tigelle can be filled with anything, and can even be found serving the role of a sandwich bread for lunch. But the typical way to eat tigelle is with a plate of cured meats, and perhaps with a selection of cheeses and pickled vegetables.

The best way to enjoy tigelle is to spread Modenese pesto inside. Generally, most people think about pesto as the green, basil-based pasta sauce from Genoa. But the word *pesto* really means anything ground. In Emilia Romagna, pesto is made with cured pancetta or lard, garlic, and rosemary. It looks like a bowl of raw pork, and can turn people off a bit, but give it a shot. When spread onto warm tigelle, the pesto starts to melt. It should also be sprinkled with grated cheese. It's possible to find something similar in Piacenza, a *gras pist*, or pounded lard, which is flavored with coarsely cut white garlic and parsley. (Speaking of Piacenza, *burtleina* is an entirely different type of meat bread that has more of a consistency of a crepe, which is often served with salumi and a selection of cheeses.)

Further to the east, traveling into Romagna, *piadina* becomes the bread of choice. Piadina is distinctly Romagnolo, and has been referred to as the bread of the people of Romagna. It is one of only two IGP breads in Emilia Romagna.

Piadina can be confused with tigelle, at first glance, as it is also a flat bread. But piadina is a lot larger and often cut into four wedges, rather than served whole like tigelle. Piadina is thinner, and there is no flower design pressed into the bread. Piadina is more crumbly, particularly after it cools. It's best to eat a piadina no more than three minutes after it cooks, which can be a challenge. It's also the case that a piadina might be prepared differently depending on which part of Romagna it is made in.

Piadina is flattened with a rolling pin and traditionally cooked on a terracotta plate on a fire. In current times, piadina is cooked on a cast-iron plate. The outside of the piadina is often spotted with dark marks from the heat, similar to a pizza crust.

It's said that piadina is best served warm with foods that can melt, including thin meats and soft cheeses. A great way to eat piadina is with squacquerone, a very soft and mild cheese that melts onto the warmed bread. The holy trinity of a piadina is to include a slice of prosciutto, a schmear of squacquerone, and a bit of rocket, or arugula. Similar to gnocco fritto, and even tigelle, it's possible to eat piadina as a dessert. But if you ask a traditionalist, they might say eating piadina with Nutella is almost a crime.

The nomenclature of meat breads can be confusing. In and around Modena, the deep fried bread that looks a little like a pillow is called gnocco fritto, and the small round bread is called tigelle or crescentine. In and around Bologna, the deep fried bread is called *crescentina*, and the small round bread is called tigelle. In Parma, the deep fried bread is called *torta fritta*. In Romagna, it's possible to find deep fried bread called *piadina frita*. In Piacenza, salumi is often served with *chisolini*, a deep fried bread fritter. Or, in Piacenza, salumi could be served with Modenese gnocco fritto, Bolognese crescentina, or Parmense torta fritta. See what I mean?

It's as though a translator is needed just to understand the starter menu in each of the subregions of Emilia Romagna. Just remember that regardless of the nomenclature, whatever you order will likely be fresh and delicious.

It should be noted that both tigelle and piadina are usually made with pork lard, so it is not a vegetarian friendly bread. Some restaurants offer vegetarian versions that are made with olive oil instead, but if you are a stickler, it's better to avoid the tigelle and piadina altogether.

There is one more bread that needs mention: Coppia Ferrarese, another IGP bread made in Emilia Romagna. Also made with lard, along with flour, malt, and olive oil, it is a twisted sourdough bread common in Romagna. Made in Ferrara, in the north of Romagna, Coppia Ferrarese is made in an "x" shape, making it the most distinctly shaped of the Emilia Romagna meat breads.

How to Taste Italian Cured Meats in Emilia Romagna

The best place to start to understand the world of Italian cured meats is at the Museo della Salumeria, outside of Modena. Even if you are not a fan of museums, this is where an exception is certainly warranted.

Villani Salumi began operations in 1886 in Castelnuovo Rangone. They started by marketing meat products and then moved into their production of salami, coppa, mortadella, and other meats. The family owned and operated company also learned about cured meats throughout Italy, not merely those produced in Emilia Romagna. It is with this history that the Villani Salumi company opened the museum in 2013.

The result? Three floors dedicated to the "art of charcuterie." From the flavors and smells of cured meats, to the history of the manufacturing process, to an entire section dedicated to the pig. Next door to the museum is the Villani Salumi food store, where you can taste various types of meats, and purchase meat souvenirs. Although Villani Salumi is not considered an artisan producer (as they produce on a mass scale) they do provide a history and education that is worth experiencing.

Museo della Salumeria, operated by Villani Salumi, Via Zanasi Eugenio, 24, 41051, Castelnuovo Rangone (MO). The museum is open daily, but closed for holidays throughout the year. Entrance to the museum is €3, a guided tour is €7. Guided tours must be booked at least three days before via email. Tasting at the Villani food shop after the tour is an additional €7. (http://www.museodellasalumeria.it/en/)

Two additional meat related museums are operated as part of Parma's Musei dei Cibo (www.museidelcibo.it). The first is a museum dedicated to Prosciutto di Parma. Referred to as "The Ham Museum," the museum is located in the heart of Langhirano, as part of the restored Foro Boario complex. The museum is home to eight different themed sections, highlighting photographs, historical documents, and machinery that tell the story of the breeds of pig used to make Prosciutto di Parma and the historic production techniques. The museum also highlights the importance of the role of the Parma Ham Consortium.

The second museum in the province of Parma is the Salami Museum in Felino, just south of Parma. Starting with the earliest document referencing salami, dated in 1436, the museum analyzes the history and tradition of salami in the region. Uniquely, the Salami Museum discusses the history of butchery and the home production of sausages, which just doesn't happen with prosciutto or culatello.

Both museums are open weekends from March 1 through December 8 from 10:00 am to 6:00 pm, and on weekdays by appointment. The Salami Museum closes for lunch on weekends, between 1:00 pm and 3:00 pm.

There are also festivals held throughout the year by the various consortia for each of the DOP and IGP meats, which are discussed in Part III.

4

TRADITIONAL BALSAMIC VINEGAR

Balsamic vinegar, aged balsamics, and balsamic glazes have been the rage recently in the States and Europe. A whole range of different balsamic vinegars are available in super markets and gourmet deli stores. You can use it to dress a salad, drizzle it over a nice chunk of cheese, or even use it to make desserts and cocktails.

However, most people don't know how much actually goes into the process of making the real stuff – the *Aceto Balsamico Tradizionale di Modena*, or traditional balsamic. The tradition and history, the process, the aging, the certification, and the tasting. In Emilia Romagna, it's possible to learn an amazing amount about these tiny bottles filled with sweet balsamic. You'll never look at balsamic vinegar the same way again.

Aceto Balsamico Tradizionale di Modena DOP

The first step to understanding traditional balsamic is to understand the production process. There is a big difference between the process of turning grapes into wine, versus grapes into balsamic. Moreover, there is a difference between grapes that become *aceto di vino* and the grapes that become balsamic. Aceto di vino is the more common vinegar that people might use in a salad. Traditional balsamic, though, is completely different.

In order to make traditional balsamic, grape juice is heated on a fire, and cooked in open air for about 24 hours. It is allowed to evaporate up to 60%. Initially, about 100 kilograms of grapes are used to produce about 75 liters of liquid, or must. After the heating process, only 35 liters remain. This evaporation results in a much thicker end product.

Eventually, the reduced liquid is placed into a series of a minimum of five barrels, called a *batteria*. Each barrel is made of a different type of wood. The batteria is where the real history, tradition, and flavor characteristics of balsamic lies. It is where the traditional balsamic goes to age.

Whereas many wines are aged in oak barrels, there is little correlation between the aging process for wine and the aging process for balsamic. In this instance, there is a batteria, a group of five barrels, each one of a different size. Each barrel is smaller than the one next to it, with the youngest balsamic held in the largest of the barrels, and the oldest in the smallest. The barrels within the batteria must be made of different types of wood. Producers can use woods such as cherry, juniper, oak, mulberry, or chestnut. The different types of wood add to the flavor characteristics of that particular traditional balsamic, as well as the color and aroma of the final product.

The process of aging the traditional balsamic vinegar is similar to the stages of schooling. The largest barrel is like elementary school, then middle school, high school, university, and finally a masters program. Not everyone who graduates high school will graduate university, and only a few people graduate with a masters degree.

Similarly, only a small amount of balsamic makes its way to the smallest barrel in the batteria. The aging process involves the transferring of the vinegar from the largest to the smallest over time. Each level of schooling produces fewer and fewer graduates, just as each barrel produces a smaller and smaller amount of traditional balsamic vinegar. The increasingly smaller amounts are due to the evaporation that occurs, which makes the balsamic more dense and more sweet over time. This process occurs over the span of 12 years, or 25 years, or sometimes longer.

Historically, almost every family in Modena would have had a batteria for making their own balsamic. When a new child was born to the family, a new batteria would be christened, along with the baby. That batteria would then be gifted to the child on their wedding day, as part of a dowry. The couple would provide small bottles of that balsamic as gifts to wedding guests. The businesses that produce balsamic do so in very similar ways, just on a larger scale.

Businesses who produce balsamic usually have done so for generations, in an *acetaia*, the place where balsamic is made. Whereas a family might maintain a few batteria for family use, an acetaia might have dozens of batteria, with possibly hundreds of individual barrels. They are all stored in the attic, where there is the greatest change in temperature over the seasons. The variations in climate throughout the year also affects the aging process, and ultimately the taste of the balsamic.

The Final Product – Aceto Balsamico Tradizionale di Modena

Remember that 100 kilograms turned into 75 liters, then into 35 liters? In the end, a single liter emerges from the smallest barrel in the batteria. After 12 or 25 years of work, from 100 kilograms of grapes, the result is maybe one liter (or a quarter of a gallon) of aged Aceto Balsamico Tradizionale di Modena DOP. And that is why true balsamic is so expensive.

The consortium that regulates Balsamico di Modena sets the standards in the region. There are two DOP versions of Modenese balsamic. Aceto Balsamico Tradizionale di Modena *Affinato* (or aged), must be a minimum of 12 years. Aceto Balsamico Tradizionale di Modena *Extra Vecchio* (or extra old), must be aged a minimum of 25 years.

The consortium also dictates the rules for bottling and labeling the two DOP products. Each balsamic producer provides a sample to the consortium for testing. The producer will also provide their label design, subject to strict DOP labeling restrictions. The consortium then bottles the vinegar, labels the bottles, and returns them to the producer for sale. The involvement of the consortium in the bottling process ensures that all producers use the exact same shaped bottle, with the same color top, either orange or gold, depending on the age. This helps the consumer distinguish between the DOP product and lesser-quality vinegars.

Producers are not allowed to print anywhere on the label that the balsamic is 12 or 25 years old. They are only permitted to say whether it is tradizionale affinato or tradizionale extra vecchio.

This is because the aging process does not allow an acetaia to know for sure the vintage of the vinegar, like a wine. There is so much mixing and transferring, that all they can say is "at least" 12, or "at least" 25 years old. Even then, you will never see the years listed on the label.

Other, cheaper balsamic may seem better than table vinegar from the supermarket, but unless it is approved by the consortium, there is no way of knowing its quality. It may include sugars, or caramel, or other additives to make it sweeter or thicker, or to give it the right color. Many tourist shops around Emilia Romagna will sell balsamic vinegar and call it Balsamico di Modena. They may even add product numbers, or lot numbers, to make it seem official. But if it is not in the official bottle, with the official consortium seal, it is not the official black gold of Aceto Balsamico Tradizionale di Modena DOP.

A 150 Year Tradition of Balsamic Vinegar

One of the oldest and most distinguished acetaia in Modena is Acetaia Pedroni. The history of Acetaia Pedroni is undeniable. Giuseppe Pedroni started an osteria, or tavern, in 1862. Since then, six generations of Pedroni men have run the osteria and their family acetaia. There has been Claudio, Cesare, Giuseppe II, Italo, and ultimately, Giuseppe III, who now works at Acetaia Pedroni alongside his father.

The quality of Acetaia Pedroni is also undeniable, with a reputation that spans the globe. When mentioning this particular acetaia to people in Emilia Romagna, locals will often smile or even roll their eyes back into their head, making an unmistakable yummy face, to let you know it is one of the best.

Although it is possible to purchase Pedroni's balsamic in their store front, and sample their vinegar, the real treat is to eat at the family's historic tavern, Osteria di Rubbiara, for a tasting and lunch that features balsamic.

Over a bottle of Pedroni Lambrusco sparkling red wine, the restaurant serves an informal yet incredible lunch. You can almost taste the tradition behind each dish. The menu changes seasonally, and sometimes weekly, although there are some standard dishes. It's a set tasting, so no menu arrives—only the dishes themselves. The meal might feature a *tortelloni*, drizzled with balsamic vinegar. Watching the balsamic pour slowly from the bottle leads to involuntary lip-smacking in anticipation. They also serve one of the best *tagliatelle* with home-made *ragù*, a traditional dish from the region.

The meat course normally includes a Lambrusco braised chicken, a recipe that apparently is a Pedroni family secret, alongside roast pork ribs, *cippollini* onions cooked in balsamic, and Acetaia Pedroni's famous balsamic vinegar omelet.

Dessert varies, but often includes a vanilla ice cream drizzled with Acetaia Pedroni balsamic vinegar, the Giuseppe Extravecchio, aged at least 25 years. Along with dessert, as is the custom throughout the region, a bottle or two of Pedroni's regional liquors might be placed on the table. This can include *nocino*, or other speciality liquors from Emilia Romagna.

A visit to Acetaia Pedroni is a must-do for foodies visiting the region, it is a special experience to have a meal where you can taste the tradition of balsamic vinegar, and the generational pride behind the business.

The Other Balsamic Vinegars of Emilia Romagna

Just like with Prosciutto di Parma, Prosciutto di Modena, and Prosciutto di San Daniele, there are other versions of balsamic vinegar produced in Emilia Romagna.

Aceto Balsamico Tradizionale di Reggio Emilia DOP is a similar DOP product, produced just west of Modena. It has its own consortium, unique rules, and regulations. The easiest way to tell the difference between the two DOP versions is in the bottling. Whereas DOP from Modena is always sold in one of two bottles, but with different labeling, the DOP from Reggio Emilia is sold in three bottles. The *aragosta*, or lobster, is aged at least 12 years, the *argento*, or silver, is aged at least 18 or 19 years, and *oro*, or gold, is aged at least 25 years.

As an alternative to the DOP versions, there is also an Aceto Balsamico di Modena IGP. Aceto Balsamico di Modena IGP is a less expensive version of balsamic than the Balsamico di Modena DOP. But, what is the difference? Generally, a DOP certification requires that the producer adhere to very particular, traditional methods. For an IGP product, the only requirement is that at least one of the phases of production needs to occur within a certain geographic area.

The IGP version guarantees that the balsamic is produced in Modena, according to the consortium's regulations. However, this balsamic does not rise to the level of the two DOP versions, as the producers may use different types of grapes, or even fermented juice or wine, to form the base of the vinegar. The entire aging process occurs in one barrel, rather than the transfer of the vinegar from one barrel to another over time. Also, for the IGP version, the vinegar must be aged a minimum of 60 days. That's a big difference! Although the producers still must be certified by the IGP consortium, producers are allowed creativity in the bottling and marketing, unlike the strict rules for the DOP product.

How to Properly Taste Aceto Balsamico Tradizionale di Modena DOP

Wine tastings, whisky tastings, gin tastings, craft beer tastings. They are all really popular and increasingly easier to find. But what about balsamic vinegar tasting? There's an art to it, and you can take part in many acetaia in Emilia Romagna.

Once you learn about real balsamic vinegar, you come to appreciate the thickness and the sweetness of a good, aged balsamic. But there should also be an acidity to the flavor because, after all, it is a vinegar. The tastings often start with a supermarket quality vinegar, and move up in quality from there. Each balsamic vinegar tastes a little sweeter than the last, and feels a little thicker on the tongue.

In Modena, you will learn that tasting balsamic vinegar involves a whole lot more than just taking a lick off a spoon.

Helena at Yummy Italy is an expert on Italian food and wines, and also a certified balsamic vinegar taster—which, of course, is a thing in Emilia Romagna. Many people think they don't have a very fine palette, but like with anything else, training of the palette is needed to understand the differences. Helena has a very refined palette, and is one of the only people who can arrange a proper balsamic tasting, like the professionals.

Acetaie across Modena will offer simple tastings. They will provide a plastic spoon and walk you through some of their offerings, hoping you will purchase a bottle. They might explain some information about the history of traditional balsamic, or how it is produced. But nothing comes close to the tasting offered by Helena. She brings small groups into an acetaia, sits them at a table with a pencil and tasting notes, and then conducts blind tastings of the balsamic. It's unlike any traditional balsamic tasting experience in Modena, and is perfect for hard core food lovers.

When tasting balsamic, it is important to only use a plastic or ceramic spoon. (Any kind of metal spoon will change the flavor of the vinegar by oxidizing it.) After pouring a taste of balsamic onto the plastic spoon, you put the spoon in your mouth, turn it over, and allow the vinegar to dissolve onto the tongue. Then, pinch the nose, hold your breath, and just as you are about to swallow, release your nose, breathe in and swallow at the same time.

Easy, right?

Who the heck came up with these convoluted balsamic tasting steps anyway?

"Scientists," according to Helena.

You can describe the taste of the balsamic using three tasting criteria. Similar to tasting wine, tasting balsamic involves a visual analysis, an olfactory (smell) analysis, and a taste analysis.

Each of these categories involves a complicated multi-step

analysis of the vinegar's density, viscosity, intensity, persistence, body, acidity, etc. Within each of these descriptors there are five choices, so that when tasting the "harmony" of the vinegar, you choose between mature, well-balanced, unbalanced, lacking, or absent.

The amazing thing is that when Helena teaches you how to properly taste balsamic, it is a truncated version of the process the consortium uses to taste and certify balsamic vinegar as an official DOP product. Hers is the easier version, despite its complexities.

All in, there are 13 different qualities, each with five rankings. Tasters receive a paper with 65 squares, along with a conclusory category describing the overall sensation. It is a bit overwhelming, but fascinating.

Unlike other balsamic vinegar tastings, which generally start with supermarket balsamic, Helena starts with the extravecchio balsamic vinegar, at least 25 years old. The 25 year old is the benchmark, as it is the ideal balsamic vinegar.

While tasting, she talks about the complex tasting chart. Once the tasting begins, it is hard not to notice there is more to high-quality balsamic vinegar than sweetness and thickness. That seems almost too obvious when you start with supermarket vinegar and move up. But by using the 25 year balsamic as a benchmark, it is easier to distinguish the complicated layers. Instead of just sweetness and thickness, there should be a balance between sweetness and acidity.

There is a complexity in analyzing the color and thickness of the vinegar as well. Placing the small jars of balsamic in front of a candle allows you to see the legs of the vinegar as the jar is swirled, similar to looking at the legs in a glass of wine.

As the tasting progresses, Helena ensures that her guests can start to tell the difference between the varieties of balsamic, including a *riserva*, which can be over 120 years old. It is certainly a unique culinary experience.

How to Visit an Acetaia

The best way to learn the secrets of Aceto Balsamico Tradizionale di Modena DOP is to tour an acetaia, or a producer of traditional balsamic. It is best to select an acetaia ahead of time, and to contact them to make a booking and ensure they're open to visitors. Basic tours will vary depending on the producer. Some just offer tastings; others will talk with you until the sun sets. But to really learn about the process, it's best to work with a culinary tour provider like Yummy Italy.

After learning so much about the fascinating process of producing traditional balsamic, many will want to take some home. The registered and regulated Aceto Balsamico Tradizionale di Modena DOP, the good stuff, generally sells for 50 Euros for affinato and 80 Euros, or more, for extravecchio. Not an investment easily made, but definitely worth the money if you really, really want to treat yourself to a little piece of luxury.

Anything cheaper than these prices, or sold in a bottle that is not labeled by the consortium, is not the real deal.

Acetaia La Noce

La Noce is run by a lovely gentleman named Giorgio, just outside of Maranello, the home of Ferrari. He teaches visitors the basics of how to make traditional balsamic vinegar. La Noce is not only an acetaia but also a museum in which Giorgio will school visitors, literally, by walking them through the production process on a blackboard.

La Noce, Via Giardini Nord, 9764, Montagnana (MO). (http://www.lanoce.it/en/)

A visit to the acetaia and balsamic vinegar tasting room is free, and Giorgio has a restaurant across the road, but reservations are required to dine, contact info@lanoce.it.

Villa San Donnino

Drive past the historic, Art Deco style home and down the gravel driveway to find the acetaia and tasting room of San Donnino. In addition to high quality DOP balsamic, Davide is also finding ways to make balsamic more approachable to food travelers, including offering a taste on fresh gelato at the end of a tour. If you ask nicely.

Villa San Donnino, Strada Medicina 25, 41126, San Donnino (MO). Although Villa San Donnino is open for tasting from 9-12:30 pm and 2-5:30 pm most days, advanced booking is recommended. It's possible to make a booking directly on their website. (http://www.villasandonnino.it/)

Acetaia Pedroni

Acetaia Pedroni and the Osteria di Rubbiara, Via Risaia, 4, Rubbiara di Nonantola, 41015 (MO). The tavern serves lunch most days between 12 and 3, and is open for dinner Friday and Saturday nights. Reservations are required.

(http://www.acetaiapedroni.it/en/storia/)

Traditional Balsamic Vinegar Museum in Spilamberto

In Spilamberto, visit the Traditional Balsamic Vinegar Museum and learn about all the stages involved in the making of this historic food product. Through a series of rooms, the museum presents the history, tradition, and regulation of balsamic vinegar. In particular, the museum sheds light on the Consortium of Traditional Balsamic and how they taste the balsamic vinegar in order to provide the DOP designation.

Traditional Balsamic Vinegar Museum, Via Roncati 28, 41057, Spilamberto (MO). The museum is open Tuesday through Sunday from 9:30-1:00 pm and 3-7:00 pm. A few times a year, the museum works with the community to offer balsamic vinegar open houses, including one the second week in April and in early October.

(http://www.museodelbalsamicotradizionale.org/ita/)

5

TRUFFLES

Perhaps no other food product is so ugly to the eye, yet so pleasant to the nose—while also being so hard on the wallet—as the world-famous truffle, or *tartufo* in Italian. And Emilia Romagna is one of the best places in the world to eat, and experience, truffles.

There are only a handful of places in the world that are known for truffles. Although truffles have been found in Europe, Asia, North America, and even North Africa, there are only a few different types of truffles that are commercially relevant. In Europe, there are black truffles from Southwest France. There are white truffles from nearby Alba, in the Piedmont area of Italy, outside of Turin, and black truffles from Umbria. Then, there are the white and black truffles of Emilia Romagna.

Truffles are found growing close to the roots of trees, generally in dark and moist areas. The truffles themselves are dark, round, bulbous, and, yes, ugly. The word truffle comes from the Latin word for tuber, or lump. It's one expensive lump. When sliced in half, the insides appear marbled and layered. Concentric circles and lines looking like veins wind themselves through the truffle.

Truffles are not really a fungus in the same way as a mushroom. Both truffles and mushrooms "grow" from spores. But truffles remain subterranean, under the soil. Mushrooms grow out of the soil, and are easier to spot. The main difference is that truffles work in symbiosis with the tree, while mushrooms do not.

The truffle spores tend to pollinate areas surrounding particular trees, including hazelnut, chestnut, and oak. Each tree variety will provide different nutrients and minerals that will affect the taste and aroma of the truffle. The tree works in symbiosis with the truffle, they each need one another. As truffles are hunted, the spores from the truffles continue to spread and pollinate around the tree.

There are a few varieties of truffles that grow in Emilia Romagna, and each has its own season. The white truffle, *tartufo bianco pregiato*, or tuber magnum, is hunted in the fall. The "100 days of White Truffle" runs from October through December. The *tartufo nero pregiato*, or tuber melanosporum, is a black truffle that is found from the end of October until March. This means the black truffle is found for more months than the white truffle, although there is an overlap in the seasons.

The March Truffle, called *marzaiolo* in Italian, is in season from February to April. It is not as aromatic as the white truffle, and is normally smaller in size. Lastly, the black summer truffle, or *scorzone* in Italian, is in season from late spring to late summer.

The start of autumn is the beginning of prime season for the esteemed white truffle in Emilia Romagna. The white truffle thrives in more humid climates. Seasons with a lot of rainfall are great for the truffle crop, therefore, prices can decrease significantly compared to drier seasons. During a good season white truffles will sell for about 80 Euros per 100 grams, although everything is dependent on the season and the weather.

Due to the increased rarity of truffles from the most famous areas, it is now common to cultivate truffles, to essentially create an environment in which truffles grow. Truffle farmers are starting to do this all over Europe, in North America, and even as far away as Tasmania. The farmers grow the trees that are needed to create the ideal elements for a truffle to grow. The ground is essentially inoculated with truffle spores. Many would say that their quality is not as high as the naturally forming truffles found in the Italian hills or from France.

Truffle Hunting

In Europe, truffles are found by following female pigs, or truffle dogs, as they hunt for the delicacy. In Emilia Romagna, truffle hunters use dogs which are able to recognize the smell of truffles underneath the surface dirt. It's more common for dogs to be used because they can be trained to find the truffle, but not eat it. The same cannot be said for truffle-hunting pigs, which seem to like the truffles as much as gourmet foodies. Additionally, the Italian government prohibits the use of pigs for truffle hunting.

The best season for quality truffle hunting in Emilia Romagna runs from early fall to spring, during the colder, rainier months of the year. It's also possible to go truffle hunting over the summer, for the summer black truffle, if the spring brought rainy weather. There are a few villages in the hills outside of Bologna where truffle hunting is possible. The best place to experience truffle hunting, though, is in the tiny town of Savigno, the *Città del Tartufo* or City of Truffles, where you can arrange a truffle hunting tour, to follow a truffle hunter and his dog for a few hours.

Using the word "city" to describe Savigno is a bit of a misnomer. At its heart, Savigno is a small village with a town square in the middle. There are a handful of cafes and even fewer restaurants. But it is known for truffles, and that is what matters.

Truffle hunting experiences generally leave from Savigno. The truffle hunter will take you into the moist and dense forest in the nearby countryside. It is only after you've spent a few hours in a forest chasing a dog around that you can truly appreciate why truffles are as expensive as they are.

The area around Savigno produces various types of truffles, including white and black, as well as the black spring truffle. Depending on the season, and the recent weather, a typical truffle hunting tour will focus on finding only one type. In the dark and humid forested areas, it's common to find the more esteemed white truffle.

One of the reasons why puppies are good to train as truffle dogs is that the hunters teach them about non-edible truffles first. Then they move onto the distinction between the edible and non-edible truffles. As the dogs grow up, they are taught to seek out the different types of truffles (white, black, spring, and summer).

As the spores develop into truffles, they start to produce an odor that is recognized by the trained dogs. Truffles are only edible for a limited time, before they're past their prime. (They won't kill you, but they might be slightly toxic.) So the key is to find the truffle when it starts to give off its characteristic odor, but before it goes bad. Because the truffle starts to give off its scent as it ripens, or matures, the truffle-hunting dog might not smell anything one day, but find a great truffle the following day, or even later that same day.

The key to truffle hunting success is a well-trained dog and a good relationship between the truffle-hunting dog and the truffle hunter, or, *tartufaio*. The dogs are rewarded for good behavior when they find a truffle. For this reason, dogs are trained to dig into the ground wherever they sense an odor, and they willingly exchange their truffle-treasure for a piece of bread and a pat on the head. Not a bad trade for the truffle hunter!

Once discovered, truffles can be collected in subsequent years at the same site. Another key to successful truffle hunting is to head towards trees that have produced truffles in the past. Because in truffle hunting, where there's one, there's more!

During a day of truffle hunting, it's possible to experience the exchange between a real tartufaio and his dog, which is an incredibly special sight. Although many of the truffle hunters prefer not to take tourists with them on a hunt, or if they do, they don't share a lot about the process. It seems they are concerned about competition, perhaps believing the tourists are potential truffle farmers. There can be big rewards, but it is not easy work. It is a long-term project: training puppies, caring for dogs, walking out in the woods in all kinds of weather. Some days are very successful, whereas it can be just as likely that they are unsuccessful.

Heading out on a truffle-hunting journey, you never know what you might find. Sometimes the dog may only find some small, edible truffles, or ones past their prime – inedible and smelly. Don't be disappointed if you do not strike gold. Often the dog can be a bit distracted by the presence of tourists. It is still a fun learning experience that will make you truly appreciate and understand the process, and why truffles are so expensive.

Dining on Truffles in Emilia Romagna

A food-focused trip through Emilia Romagna can involve a lot of luxury dining, the kind that marries tradition with modern techniques, while using fresh local ingredients. When planning a trip, you will undoubtedly come across Michelin Star this and Michelin Star that. This is particularly true with Chef Massimo Bottura's Osteria Francescana in Modena, which nailed the title of "Best Restaurant in the World" in 2016—according to The World's 50 Best.

If you want a true truffle dining experience, though, look no further than the famous Trattoria Amerigo in (where else?) Savigno, the City of Truffles. Only a 30-minute drive from bustling Bologna, peaceful Savigno is like walking into a whole different world.

When thinking about dining at a Michelin Star restaurant in a town known as the City of Truffles, you might expect something out of a Hollywood blockbuster, something fancy, where you would immediately feel underdressed. Not exactly black tie, but Italians dressed to the nines and fancy, pompous servers.

Instead, Amerigo is down to earth, almost like a warm and welcoming country house. Yes, the food is served on white tablecloths on china rimmed with gold, but underneath are the traditional red checkered ones of days past. If you look beyond the gold rimmed china, Amerigo seems like a neighborhood restaurant, filled with locals out for some classic Italian fare.

Just through the bar area is a shop specializing in local products, including their own brand of jams and sauces. A great selection of uber-local wines, almost all of which come from the neighboring Bologna Hills wineries, adorns one wall. By entering the restaurant through the shop, it is immediately apparent that Amerigo's focus is on quality local products.

As much as the decor of this Michelin Star restaurant is simple and rustic, there is one part of the dining experience that can certainly be deemed decadent. If you choose the tartufo tasting, the meal is focused on truffles. And not just the regular old black truffle, but the good stuff served in the right season—the expensive stuff: Italian white truffles. Loads of it. All served by Chef-Patron Alberto Bettini and sourced locally, the result of truffles hunts in and around Savigno. More often than not,

Alberto serves his guests, or walks around the dining room to chat with the locals. He is definitely a presence at the little restaurant.

To truly enjoy truffles, it's important to eat them as fresh as possible, shortly after they've been harvested. Thus, there is something to be said for eating truffles at a restaurant where the truffles came from less than a 10-minute drive away. Talk about zero-kilometer dining! It's also important to visit the restaurant in the correct season: For white truffles, it is best to visit during the 100 Days of White Truffles. Although Alberto serves truffles throughout the year, he will only use white truffles when they are at their freshest.

The menu at Amerigo is focused on tradition, bringing in not only local truffles but other fresh, local ingredients. Alberto sources his eggs locally. The flour for the pasta comes from a historic, local flour mill. He is proud of the meats he serves, and knows the pigs and cows are of the highest quality. He carefully selects these ingredients from trusted farmers and producers to prepare his menu.

Amerigo's menu includes *pancotto*, a traditional dish in the region. Instead of pasta, day-old bread is used. It is soaked, and layered with *béchamel* sauce, and mushrooms to make a poor man's lasagna. It is simply amazing...creamy, earthy, and an intense way to begin a multi-course meal.

The beef tartare is made using the meat from the local white Modenese cow, and it is loaded with truffles. The fresh, tender meat is mixed with local, extra virgin olive oil from Romagna. It melts in the mouth, and the aroma of the truffles is to die for. This dish alone is worthy of the drive from Bologna.

Be sure to try the passatelli with white truffles. Passattelli is a dense, rolled pasta, which is slightly doughy, and textured enough to grab onto the surrounding sauces. The texture comes from all of the Parmigiano Reggiano and breadcrumbs that are used to make the pasta itself, and is also the reason it's so delicate.

At many restaurants, you can expect a white truffle pasta course to involve one, maybe two, slivers of truffles; Alberto believes in going all in. You can barely see the pasta under the layers of white truffles. (Most restaurants tend to use about seven grams of truffles in a dish, whereas Alberto uses 10 grams.) In the winter, he offers a passatelli with a liver ragù—usually with black truffle—as an alternative.

Next up is the *oi al tartufo,* a thick and creamy gnocchi served with, what else, truffles. Although black truffles have both a smell and a taste, white truffles do not necessarily have a unique taste of their own. The intrigue of the white truffles comes from the smell. Start each of these courses with your nose deep in the dish, taking it all in. Truffles add richness to a dish, even one that is already rich, like a plate of large potato gnocchi. Alberto also offers a white lasagna, made with a white ragù, that is, of course, loaded with truffles. His white ragù is made from the famous local Mora Romagnolo black pig.

Of all these dishes, one of Amerigo's most famous is the white truffle egg. Each year, Alberto develops a new version of the truffle egg. One year, his truffle egg involved beating egg whites, then cooking them in an oven, while allowing the yolk to stay liquid inside.

To make the dish, egg whites are whipped up, almost to the point of a meringue consistency. The fluffed egg whites are placed inside a metal tin, similar to a large, single muffin tin. A deep orange egg yolk is placed inside of each tin, and additional egg whites are placed on top, making a muffin-shaped concoction.

After baking them for just a few minutes, the warmed egg dish is topped with layers upon layers of decadent white truffles. At the table, a knife is used to cut into the truffle egg, where you'll expose the layers of bright white and golden yellow, as the egg yolk spreads onto the plate. It is almost like an egg white muffin, covered in white truffles. A side dish to the truffle egg is another white truffle egg, with the second one wrapped inside potato and covered with truffles.

The first time we dined at Amerigo, we were joined by Chef Amy Ferguson, a well-known chef in Hawaii. After the giant platter, with two kinds of truffle eggs, was placed in front of us, Chef Ferguson looked at me across the table. We knew we were done for the night. Four carb-heavy courses preceded, three of which were covered in truffles, left a decadent odor of earthy truffle dangling over our table. My belly was filled with fantastic local wines, pasta, and truffles, and I wanted to cry, "Mercy!"

I am never one to shy away from food, but even before I dug a fork into the white truffle egg I knew we had one more pasta course to go. As a mere non-chef mortal, I was hesitant to inform Chef Bettini that I could not eat another bite, let alone another course of pasta. These were not small servings, either. I implored Chef Ferguson to give notice of our intention to call mercy—a cry from one chef to another—stating that we could not go any further.

There was some disappointment in Chef Bettini's eyes as we passed on the tagliatelle al tartufo. Instead, we continued with some after-dinner grappa, and a gelato to aid in digestion, and passed out, literally, right across the street.

Although we were staying in an agriturismo about 45 minutes drive from Savigno, we actually booked a last-minute room at the one hotel in town with a room, across the street from Amerigo. We knew it would be too late, and Eric would be in too much of a food coma, to drive home. This was the first time we have ever done this: walked away from a hotel room, and paid for another, due to overeating. I was so glad we did.

Dinner started well after 8pm and did not end until close to 11. Three hours of white truffles and traditional Italian food and wine. But it was worth it. There is such a thing as too much truffles!

Chef Bettini: well done, sir.

Grazie for the truffle egg that did us in.

Amerigo dal 1934

Amerigo dal 1934, Via Marconi, 14-16, Savigno (BO). The restaurant suggests not using your GPS to find them, because the GPS is wrong! Call ahead, or look just off the main square in Savigno for the storefront. Open for lunch, only with reservations. Open for dinner most nights. Reservations are recommended by emailing or calling. The white truffle dishes at Amerigo are approximately 35 Euros, but other, non-truffle dishes can be had for a lot less. The menu is only in Italian, but Alberto, or his wife, can help explain. (http://www.amerigo1934.it/index.php)

Helena from Yummy Italy can arrange a truffle hunting experience in Savigno as part of a truffle-filled day. (http://www.yummy-italy.com/the-famous-truffle-hunt).

The town of Savigno hosts a truffle festival in November. White truffles are also found in Sant'Agata Feltria in Rimini, which hosts a fall white truffle festival in October. It's possible to arrange truffle-hunting excursions there as well.

6

PASTA

Thus far, we've talked about so many of the DOP and IGP products that are produced in Emilia Romagna, many of which are specific to the region and nowhere else. But, many people travel to Italy in search of one thing: the best pasta in the world.

If you grew up in the U.S. or Europe, you probably ate pasta all the time. Especially in the States, that pasta would come in a box. On special occasions, perhaps a splurge on some fresh pasta from the deli counter would be warranted. Normally these pasta purchases focused on the most commonly known varieties, such as ravioli, lasagna, and, of course, spaghetti.

When you're in Italy, however, there are so many more varieties. This is especially the case in Emilia Romagna pasta, where pasta is usually made with egg. Sure, there will be some pasta dishes that look familiar, but then there are others that will be brand spanking new. Most important, there won't be a single plate of spaghetti bolognese in sight. It's not a dish that exists in Italy.

Emilia Romagna Pasta Dishes

Tortelloni

Tortelloni

One of the pasta dishes that will be most familiar to Americans is tortelloni, a small half-moon shaped pasta pinched at one end. They are generally stuffed with cheese or meat. In Emilia, it is common to find tortelloni in a cream sauce, or slathered in butter and topped with sage.

Another version that's commonly served in Emilia, which is very popular, is tortelloni drizzled with aged balsamic vinegar, and sprinkled with local Parmigiano Reggiano cheese. The savory flavor of the pasta is offset perfectly by the sweet taste of the balsamic vinegar.

Tortellini and Tortelli

What, then, is the difference between tortelloni and *tortellini*? Or what about tortelloni and *tortelli*? This can be pretty confusing. In Italian, anytime the letters "ini" are added at the end of a word, it means smaller. Tortellini is a smaller version of tortelloni. It can also be confusing because many Italian restaurant menus in the States use the word tortellini more generically, referring to the larger version of this pasta. But, in Emilia Romagna, there is a big difference. Once you have seen how hard it is to make tortelloni just right, you can only imagine how hard it is to make them even smaller. Tortelli, on the other hand, is slightly larger than the tortelloni. Similar shapes, in three different sizes.

Tortellini

The most common way to eat tortellini is in a light broth, particularly during the winter months. This dish, *tortellini in brodo,* is also a must-eat dish for Christmas. Outside of the winter months it is common to find tortellini also in a cream sauce, although traditionalists decry brodo to be the only way to serve tortellini. And, it is almost always filled with meat, with the official recipe including a mix of pork loin, mortadella, prosciutto, Parmigiano Reggiano, salt, pepper, and nutmeg.

Tortelli comes in several shapes. The most common version looks similar to a ravioli due to its size. But it can also take a shape more similar to cappelletti, which is hat shaped. Although you can find tortelli all over Emilia Romagna, in Piacenza, it is common to find *tortelli con la coda*. This version is stuffed with ricotta cheese and spinach.

Cappelletti

In Romagna, *cappelletti* is similar to a smaller version of tortelloni. The Romagnolo version is normally stuffed with ricotta cheese along with a fresh cheese called raviggiolo. Cappelletti, which translates to "little hat," is also a typical Christmas dish served in Romagna. It's often served in a *capon* broth, made from a castrated rooster. Despite not sounding all that romantic, capon is actually more flavorful than chicken and it makes for an amazing way to eat cappelletti. Cappelletti in Ferrara, though, normally includes chicken, pork neck, veal, and a cooked salame, along with egg and Parmigiano Reggiano. Heading out of Romagna, and more towards Emilia, it is more likely to find cappelletti stuffed with meat.

Interestingly, it is sometimes hard to find these fresh pastas in Emilia Romagna during the summer. The reason? To make pasta that small takes a lot of manual dexterity. It also becomes almost impossible in the heat of summer because the pasta becomes too dry to maneuver.

Ravioli and Anolini

Although it is possible to find ravioli in Emilia Romagna, it might be more common to see tortelli or *anolini* on a menu. In Parma and Piacenza, where anolini is popular, it's often stuffed with ground beef or pork, Grana Padano, and nutmeg. In Piacenza, it is also common to serve the anolini in a "thirds" broth, made of beef, capon, and lean pork meat, and topped, of course, with local Grana Padano cheese.

To the east of Piacenza, anolini is often filled with a cheese mixture. In Monticelli, it's filled with egg, bread crumbs, and

Grana Padano. And in Castelvetro Piacentino, it would be filled with a sausage and cheese mixture.

A similar pasta, well known in Lombardy, has also crossed the border into Emilia Romagna. In this case, the pasta is referred to as *marubini*. The pasta can be shaped into round pieces or into half moons. The pasta is filled with ground salami and braised beef with Grana Padano.

Gnocchi

Another dish that has grown in popularity in recent decades in the U.S. and around the world is gnocchi, a dense, round ball made of potato. Gnocchi is made by boiling or baking potatoes, which are pressed like mashed potatoes, and then mixed with egg and flour. The mixture is then rolled out into a long, thin log and cut into smaller pieces with a pasta cutter. Those pieces are then rolled onto a cheese grater style tool, which gives the pasta some texture. This is what gives the gnocchi a little character, and also helps it to hold the pasta sauce better.

Tagliatelle

Tagliatelle is a pasta than can often be confused with many other Italian pasta shapes, including fettuccine and pappardelle, as they are each different variations of a similar pasta. Tagliatelle is made by rolling out the pasta until it is so thin you can almost see through it. Then, the pasta is cut with a knife to make it the perfect thickness.

If you accidentally make it too wide, it turns out to be pappardelle. Too thin, and it is tagliolini. Regardless of its width, in this case, it is best served in Emilia Romagna with meat ragù, a typical Bolognese sauce. Just don't call it spaghetti bolognese, a dish that does not exist in Emilia Romagna.

Tagliatelle

Passatelli

Passatelli is particular to Emilia Romagna, and virtually unheard of outside of Italy. It is a traditional pasta that is thicker than many other pastas, and has a more dense taste to it. As dense as it is, it is more delicate than it appears.

Passatelli is made with Parmigiano Reggiano, bread crumbs, egg, flour, and sometimes nutmeg. All of the ingredients are slowly folded into one another to form a dough. The mixture is run through a press, similar to a potato ricer, to form its eel-like shape. There is a texture, or a roughness, to the pasta, which allows the sauce to hold onto it more than a smooth pasta would. Part of the texture is due to the fact that no water is added into the pasta mixture, which is typical of many pasta dishes from Emilia Romagna.

Passatelli

You have to be careful when cooking passatelli at home, as it only takes about 90 seconds to cook. Even then, it can easily fall apart if you're not careful. It's best to leave the passatelli preparation to the Emilia Romagna pasta professionals, though it is getting increasingly more difficult to find on menus in Emilia Romagna because it is so expensive to make. All of that Parmigiano Reggiano adds up.

It's most common to find passatelli served in a broth, which is the traditional preparation. However, you can also find passatelli served "dry," without a broth, often mixed with fresh vegetables or meats.

Garganelli

Another pasta, which is less well-known outside of Italy, *garganelli* is made in a similar way to tagliatelle, by rolling the pasta very thin. Although it is possible to cut the pasta with a knife, a pasta roller is often used to cut the pasta into asymmetrical squares, with equally spaced small ridges.

Garganelli

Then, a *pettine* is used, which looks like the world's smallest laundry board. Pettine translates to "comb," and it looks similar to an ancient comb. The pasta is rolled around a small wooden stick, then over the little pettine to make grooves on the outside of the pasta, as a way to hold the sauce. The whole process is fairly delicate.

To an untrained eye, garganelli looks similar to what are known as rigatoni in the U.S., but garganelli is a lot softer. The space in the center that is made by the wooden stick collapses beautifully when cooked. Before serving, it's layered with sauce.

Gramigna

New travelers to Emilia Romagna might find it easy to get confused between garganelli and *gramigna* when perusing restaurant menus. Gramigna is a hollow, tube-like pasta, named after a particular type of grass. It is short, and shaped like a curlicue. It is made by running the pasta through a contraption that looks like a sausage maker, called a bronze extruder. The machine has a hand crank that extrudes the pasta, using friction.

Gramigna

The most common way to eat gramigna is with a sausage-based ragù, *gramigna alla salsiccia*. It is also possible to find gramigna in different colors, including a green spinach version.

How to Make Your Own Pasta in Emilia Romagna

Many people dream of learning how to cook Italian food, in Italy. There's something romantic about traveling to Italy, immersing yourself in the local language, and taking a series of Italian cooking classes. It would be like a personalized version of "Under the Tuscan Sun."

There's no better place to do this, though, than in Emilia Romagna. So, perhaps, it is living "Under the Emilia Romagna Sun," even if it doesn't have the same sort of ring to it. Because there is such a wide variety of unique types of pasta in the region, it really is an intriguing place to broaden your pasta horizons. After eating all of the pasta in the region, it's the perfect opportunity to roll up your sleeves and get dusted with flour during a cooking class in Emilia Romagna.

Luckily, it is not hard to find cooking classes in Emilia Romagna. From commercial kitchens to Italian *nonnas*, or grandmothers, the art of pasta making is easily shared.

Pasta Making in the Home of Italian Cooking

In Forlimpopoli lies Casa Artusi, a museum, library, and cooking school, named after the Italian gastronome, Pellegrino Artusi. Artusi is often credited as being the father of Italian food. Prior to Italian unification, each region or state within Italy had its own unique cooking style. In the late 1800s, Artusi traveled the entire country and created the first national cookbook. Artusi wasn't even a chef, or a cook, just a passionate foodie; before being one became a thing.

His book, "Science in the Kitchen and the Art of Eating Well," has been in circulation since the 1800s. It's often given to Italian brides as a wedding gift. They say if the book comes from the bride's new mother-in-law, it's not a good omen. It means the mother-in-law doesn't trust the bride to cook well.

Casa Artusi is dedicated to the concept of Italian home cooking. During a cooking class, it's possible to learn each of the famous Emilia Romagna pasta dishes. Most of the pasta dishes are made with nothing more than flour and egg, giving them a distinct yellow color. It also means the pasta is fresh and needs to be cooked and eaten quickly.

Cooking classes at Casa Artusi are run by the *Associazione delle Mariette*. The association's goal is to teach traditional forms of cooking Italian food. The Mariette, named after Marietta, Artusi's cook and housekeeper, are also all volunteers and are not paid to teach at the school. They are simply dedicated to the goals of maintaining the traditions of Italian cooking. It is an amazing experience to learn from women who have been making pasta since they were little girls.

One of the hardest parts of making fresh pasta is to roll the dough until it is a thin sheath. It requires a bit of strength and a lot of determination. Luckily, the Mariette are willing to step in to speed things along when needed. After rolling the pasta, it's time to cut the pasta, or form it into small shapes, like tiny tortellini, or rolling it into garganelli.

One thing to note, the entire pasta-making course at Casa Artusi is in Italian. But that doesn't seem to be a problem. Each Mariette will demonstrate the different pastas and help students along. Language is certainly not a barrier when you are talking about food. After all, food is a universal language.

Pasta Making In a Simple Italian Restaurant

Nonantola is a small town many people overlook when traveling to Emilia Romagna. Just outside of Modena, Nonantola is home to the famous Acetaia Pedroni, a stone's throw from town. La Piazetta Del Gusto on the town square is not owned by a famous chef. Instead, Massimo—the owner—is someone who just loves food, and he's hired the right people to make his kitchen buzz.

Most cooking classes in Emilia Romagna involve learning how to make tortelloni, stuffed with cheese. It's just such a classic pasta dish in the region. But, it is one of the hardest pastas to make because you have to stuff the delicate pasta and curl it between your fingers, pressing firmly. The pasta maker at La Piazetta Del Gusto does her best to explain the various techniques.

Unlike some of the other cooking classes, at La Piazetta Del Gusto, they teach you how to make the recommended sauces too. To make *Tortelloni Vecchia Modena*, bacon is cooked in butter. Then, the tortelloni is folded into the butter and bacon mixture. Finally, the pasta is drizzled with balsamic vinegar and topped with grated Parmigiano Reggiano. This is one of the quintessential Modenese dishes. And, it is easy to make. After a La Piazetta Del Gusto cooking class, students do actually eat their own pasta!

Pasta Making in a Family Kitchen

Some agriturismi around the region also offer cooking classes to their guests. Because many of these country farm house establishments are smaller and built on family land, it is a much more casual experience. One such experience can be had at Fattoria Maria, a small family-owned agriturismo in Soliera, outside Modena.

It's one thing to take a cooking class in a space like Casa Artusi, which is set up specifically to host cooking classes. It's another thing to take a cooking class in a professional kitchen, like at La Piazzetta. In this case, it is as though you are learning to cook in the family's kitchen, albeit one that supports a public restaurant.

Three generations walk in and out of the kitchen as the women teach pasta-making skills. The lessons might include how to roll garganelli over the pettine, which looks more like a small medieval torture device than a pasta roller. Or, how to roll out pasta for tagliatelle.

In addition to learning how to make pasta, Fattoria Maria teaches how to make gnocco fritto, the Modenese version of a puffy deep fried bread. After class, lunch is served in the agriturismo, complete with pasta, gnocco fritto with freshly sliced cured meats, and of course a bottle of Lambrusco.

How to Book the Perfect Experience

You can contact Casa Artusi directly to book their Italian cooking classes, as well as many of the agriturismo properties throughout Emilia Romagna. Look for properties that list cooking courses on their website, or email them ahead of time to see what they recommend in the surrounding area.

Casa Artusi hosts group cooking classes, but, there are also loads of opportunities to have one-on-one classes, like the experience at Fattoria Maria. The great thing about Emilia Romagna is that it has sophisticated culinary tourism offerings, where anything is possible.

Classes start at low as €60 per person, and increase in price based on class size and duration.

Casa Artusi

Their motto is "the art of eating well." Although this can be said about most establishments in the region, Casa Artusi focuses on teaching travelers the necessary skills to bring traditional Italian cooking home with them. Cooking classes are available for one to 20, and classes taught in English are possible with advanced request. They offer both demonstrations and hands-on courses, mostly on weekdays.

Casa Artusi, Via Andrea Costa, 27, Forlimpopoli (FC). Contact Casa Artusi directly to discuss options for cookery courses and demonstrations. (http://www.casartusi.it/en/)

La Piazzetta Del Gusto

La Piazzetta Del Gusto is known for its passatelli. If booking a cooking class, ask about learning to make passatelli, or at least watch a demonstration of how it is made. It's a truly unique Emilia Romagna experience.

La Piazzetta Del Gusto, Via Roma, 24, Nonantola (MO). Located just off the main square in Nonantola. Cooking classes at La Piazzetta Del Gusto can be booked through tour operator ModenaTur.

(http://www.modenatur.it/)

(http://www.lapiazzettadelgusto.com/en/)

Fattoria Maria

Also located outside of Modena, Fattoria Maria is a must visit if heading into the outskirts of Modena. Cooking courses are personalized and by arrangement only, but are simple, quaint, and worth the effort.

Fattoria Maria, Via Stradello Lama, 157-163, 41019 Soliera (MO). Cooking classes at Fattoria Maria can be booked through tour operator ModenaTur. (http://www.fattoriamaria.com/)

7

GELATO

A day is not a day in Emilia Romagna without gelato. And the gelato in Emilia Romagna is impeccable.

Gelato is everywhere in Italy. Loads of it. In bright colors. All for next to nothing. You'll see families enjoying gelato in Italy on a Sunday afternoon, and couples strolling arm-in-arm with a cone of gelato, sharing each other's flavors.

But once you start digging a bit deeper into the art of gelato making, you will realize that everything you think you know about gelato is wrong.

Well, not quite wrong, just not quite what you'd expect.

Artisan Gelato

Imagine a corner *gelateria* with a dozen or more vats of gelato in exotic flavors like Nutella, *crema*, pistachio, and *stracciatella*. The gelato is whipped and piled high in plastic tubs, often with wisps of bright red strawberry, or bright purple blueberry, peaking through. Some vats might include bright blue Smurf-like colors with rainbow colored candies. Most people select their flavors based on what looks good, but boy are they mistaken.

There is so much more to quality gelato in Italy than you might guess. There is a trend in Emilia Romagna right now where many gelateria are becoming specialists in artisan gelato. But, how do you tell whether gelato is of the highest quality; if it's what might be called "artisan" gelato?

First, an artisan gelateria will only use natural products and no artificial flavors, preservatives, or colors. With no artificial coloring or flavoring, the gelato is not going to be bright red or purple, unless it is due to fresh fruits being added. Gelato makers may freeze fresh berries in the summer for use in the fall and winter – but they will not use artificial strawberry flavor in their gelato. This means that artisan gelato is not brightly colored like you'll see elsewhere in Italy. If you see Smurf-blue gelato, it is certainly not artisan. With no artificial preservatives, it means gelato is fresh, and generally made daily. Some artisan gelato shops even have their own gelato laboratory on site!

The second clue: pay attention to how the gelato is stored in the shop. Artisan gelato makers store their gelato not in giant vats, open to the air and the elements, but deep inside the counter top, temperature controlled, and covered by a metal lid. This storage method controls the temperature so the gelato is not exposed to oxygen or light. This is particularly important because they don't use artificial preservatives. Gelato makers take their job so seriously they control the temperature within a tenth of a degree.

Last, gelato is not merely the Italian word for ice cream. There are distinct differences between the two cold treats: Gelato generally has less fat than ice cream, mostly because it is made with whole milk, whereas ice cream is made with cream. Also, American-style ice cream has a lot of air churned into the product. With gelato, there is less air so it is smoother and creamier, despite having less fat.

Attending Gelato University

When traveling in Italy, there's something about grabbing a schmear of gelato and walking gingerly on a *passeggiata* around town. It's romantic. If you love everything about gelato, it's possible to get a crash course in how to make gelato, at the Gelato University.

Carpigiani is one of the main manufacturers of ice cream machines and one of the oldest. Their headquarters is located on the Via Emilia, the food and wine route running through Emilia Romagna. They have ice cream cone art all over the walls, and even on the doors to the bathrooms. For a gelato or ice cream enthusiast, it's love at first lick.

Carpigiani also operates a gelato museum in the same building. The museum includes information on the history of ice cream, and shows off some historic gelato-related memorabilia.

For a more intense immersion, you can take a full course at

Gelato University, run by Carpigiani. It is a pretty intense affair that can run up to four weeks and cost thousands of dollars. The program is perfect for someone who is looking to open their own gelateria somewhere in the world.

Alternatively, it is possible to take a one-hour course at Gelato University, which is more manageable for the average food traveler. During the first part of the experience the gelato teacher explains all about gelato, and how it differs from ice cream, and sorbet. Then, the hands-on training begins.

There are two ways to make gelato during the demonstration. The first is gelato made by hand, using ice cold water to cool the liquid until it becomes more solid. This requires a lot of ice, and a lot of constant stirring. It's not all that practical, but demonstrates how hard it is to make gelato without one of the modern ice cream machines.

The second way includes pouring the mix into a high tech industrial gelato machine. After ten minutes or so, the machine will not only tell you the gelato is ready, but will inform you that the gelato is, indeed, excellent. Literally, the screen on the machine reads "gelato excellent" when it is complete.

As much as Carpigiani is high-tech, it is similar to the machines used by artisan gelato makers. What makes artisan gelato artisanal is the quality of the ingredients that are placed into the machine.

Then comes the hard part. Most artisan gelato makers will store their gelato inside the metal vats below the counter. But at Gelato University, they teach you how to present the gelato, in the regular above-the-counter containers. In their opinion, it is important to make the gelato look fancy, to encourage people to buy it. So a part of the course includes learning decorative gelato display skills, which is harder than it looks.

Just like any other university, the best part of attending Gelato

University is learning new skills, right? Wrong. The best part of attending Gelato University is actually getting to taste the gelato. As much as you want.

In the end, it is possible to "graduate" from Gelato University, with a diploma and everything. If you really want to open your own gelato shop, however, it would be necessary to take the full course. Still, the diploma is a great souvenir from Emilia Romagna and an interesting way to learn more about gelato.

Carpigiani Gelato University and Gelato Museum

The basic gelato workshop is called the Discovering Gelato Tour, which takes less than two hours and includes a hands-on demonstration. The Discovering Gelato Tour costs €20. A more thorough Gelato Masterclass costs €45 and lasts over three hours. Then there is the full-blown Gelato University for wannabe gelato professionals! If Gelato University is not a possibility, the museum alone is worth a visit, as it traces the history of gelato and ice cream from 12,000 B.C. to present times.

Carpigiani Gelato University and Gelato Museum, Via Emilia, 45, 40011 Anzola Emilia (BO). Carpigiani is located outside of

Bologna in Anzola dell'Emilia. The Gelato Museum is open Tuesday through Saturday, from 9:00 am – 6:00 pm, but reservations are required. (http://gelatomuseum.com/en/)

Where to Eat Gelato in Emilia Romagna

It is not hard to find gelato in Emilia Romagna, but to find the best ones it helps to have a recommendation. Remember to look for gelato kept underneath the countertops, with lids to cover the product. This is a sign of a better quality gelato. It might be harder to pick a flavor, but it is worth it.

At busier gelato shops, you might have to pay at the register, then take your receipt to the counter to actually choose your flavors. It's customary for a single gelato cup or cone to have two flavors in one. Choose wisely by selecting flavors that complement each other.

Most important: the best way to spend an eating holiday in Emilia Romagna is to secure a scoop of gelato at least once a day!

Cremeria Santo Stefano in Bologna

Set on the outskirts of the old town centre, Cremeria Santo Stefano has an almost cult-like following and is most people's first recommendation for gelato in Bologna. Artisan gelato with typical flavors, as well as flavors of the month, including *ricotta e visciole*, or ricotta cheese and sour cherry. They also offer fresh fruit flavored gelatin candies, or *gelatine*, as well as freshly baked pastries.

Cremeria Santo Stefano, Via Santo Stefano, 70, 40125 Bologna (BO).

Gelateria Galliera 49 in Bologna

Often found on lists of top gelato shops in Italy, and known for their Sicilian granita, Galliera is well known among Bologna locals for their list of traditional flavors, as well as specials, including ricotta with pear and chocolate, and a version with local nougat.

Gelateria Galliera 49, Via Galliera, 49/b, 40121 (BO). (http://www.galliera49.it/en/home-en)

Gelateria Gianni in Bologna

Centrally located, just around the corner from the Mercato delle Erbe, Gianni doesn't serve artisan gelato, but it is reliable and always busy.

Gelateria Gianni, Via Monte Grappa, 11, 40121 Bologna (BO). (https://www.facebook.com/gelateriagianni/)

Emilia Cremeria

With locations across the region including one in Modena and Parma, Emilia Cremeria is a reliable choice for gelato. Using only natural raw materials and quality ingredients, they make their gelato daily at each of their locations. Unlike other gelato "chains" they refuse to make their gelato in industrial laboratories with unnatural processes. No hydrogenated fats or artificial colorings are used.

Gelato flavors include *bacio con nocciola del Piemonte* (Piemonte hazelnuts), *biscottino con frollini al cacao* (chocolate biscuits), *cheesecake con fragole e biscotti inglesi* (strawberries and English biscuits), *fiordilatte con latte fresh biologico* (fresh, organic milk), and the famous *crema*, a gelato typical of the region. Emilia Cremeria also offers fresh and tangy granita made with Sorrento lemons. The little gelato cups in the display case are themselves works of art. Order a cone, and get a shot of warm dark chocolate in the base for a final treat.

Emilia Cremeria, Piazza Mazzini Giuseppe, 17, 41121 Modena

(MO); Str. Luigi Carlo Farini, 29, Parma (PR). (http://www.cremeriaemilia.com/)

Gelateria Bloom in Modena

Another artisan gelateria, just around the corner from Emilia Cremeria's Modena location. A little smaller, and often with a line out the door. In addition to gelato, Bloom serves Sorrento lemon granita. They have vegan options as well.

Gelateria Bloom, Via Luigi Carlo Farini, 23, Modena (MO). (https://www.facebook.com/gelateriabloom/)

Gelateria Pomposa in Modena

If staying closer to Parc Novi Sad, Gelateria Pomposa is a little neighborhood gelateria that offers amazing value and high quality gelato and granita. Flavors are written in chalk on the board, with typical flavors as well as rotating specials.

Gelateria Pomposa, Via del Voltone, 16, Modena (MO). (https://www.facebook.com/gelateria.pomposa/)

Gelateria Sanelli in Salsomaggiore Terme

Outside of Parma, this is *the* gelato shop in Salsomaggiore Terme. In a country filled with gelaterie, it was recently listed as #27 on Italy's Best Gelateria list.

Gelateria Sanelli, 2/L Piazza Del Popolo, Salsomaggiore Terme (PR).

Il Teatro del Gelato in Sant'Agostino

Listed as #75 on Italy's Best Gelateria list. Located in Ferrara, they specialize in gelato as well as granita and milkshakes. Try the mascarpone cheese or *cassata* made with cow's milk ricotta cheese and candied citrus.

Il Teatro del Gelato, Piazza Sandro Pertini, 2, 44047 Sant'Agostino (FE). (http://www.ilteatrodelgelato.com/)

Grom Gelato

A major gelato chain based in Turin, with locations as far west as . . . Hollywood. They also have locations in Emilia Romagna. Similar to Emilia Cremeria, they promise no artificial flavoring, coloring, or preservatives. Their *caramello al sale* is made with caramel and Himalayan pink salt. Or try an *affogato*, made with gelato and espresso.

There are Grom shops in Bologna, Modena, Parma, and Ferrara. (http://www.grom.it/en/)

PART II

THE WINES OF EMILIA ROMAGNA

When you think of Italian wines, what do you think of? Most often it is the Tuscan wines, like Chianti, Barolo, or Montepulciano. Maybe you think of Prosecco, or god forbid Santa Margherita Pinot Grigio. But, do you ever think about Lambrusco? Sangiovese? What about Pignoletto or Albana? Chances are you've never even heard of some of these great Italian wines.

There are so many quality wines produced throughout Emilia Romagna. Foreign varietals that grow well include Chardonnay, Sauvignon Blanc, Cabernet Sauvignon, Merlot, and Pinot Noir. But the real treat in tasting the wines of Emilia Romagna is in learning about the grapes that are most well known locally. Many of which remain a secret outside of the region. They are primed for discovery and represent the future of Italian wine tourism.

Emilia Romagna is the second-largest wine producing region in Italy, after the Veneto. Just think: it's not Tuscany, where most people associate Italian wine. In fact, Emilia Romagna is one of the oldest wine growing regions, dating back to the 7th century B.C. when the Etruscans, and later the Romans, developed wine production. This part of Italy offers a growing export market, exporting around Europe, to the United States, and even father afield.

These are small producers, who most likely still harvest by hand, using wooden carts to collect the grapes. They are pressing grapes and aging wine in their garage or their basement. They are incorporating traditional production methods from France to bring new life to ancient Italian grapes.

They are experimenting with producing wine aged in terracotta vats instead of oak or steel. The ancient Romans used terracotta to age their wine, and winemakers in Emilia Romagna are resurrecting the process. With red wines, this process offers an extremely clean and clear taste. With white wines, the vats age the wine in a way that entirely changes their primary characteristics.

On the opposite end, winemakers are using modern technology to create high-quality wines by incorporating computer-controlled presses, drone cameras, and the latest bottling techniques.

There is a little of everything when it comes to wine producers in Emilia Romagna. From family owned and operated, to larger producers. From traditional to contemporary. It is one of the reasons why the wines of Emilia Romagna are ready for tasting.

Classification of Emilia Romagna Wines

Similar to the DOP and IGP classification system for food products in Italy, wines are subject to similar rules and regulations. For wines, there are three levels of classification, DOCG (*Denominazione di Origine Controllata e Garantita*), DOC (*Denominazione di Origine Controllata*), and IGT (*Indicazione Geografica Tipica*), with DOCG being the highest and most stringent of the classifications.

Generally, DOCG wines are analyzed and tested by the regulating bodies. When the wines are certified, they receive a special seal across their cap, or more often, cork. This label is intended to prevent tampering. There are only two DOCG wine appellations (or areas) in Emilia Romagna: Albana in Romagna, and Colli Bolognesi Pignoletto Classico in the Bologna Hills.

On the other end of the spectrum, IGT wines are labeled by the location where they were produced, but don't rise to the level of DOCG, or even DOC wines. There are nine IGT wine appellations in Emilia Romagna. In between these two wine extremes are the 20 or so DOC wine appellations of Emilia Romagna. These appellations include some of the most characteristic wines of the region.

It is one thing to run through a list of the wine appellations that are either DOCG or DOC, but it is another thing to learn the story behind the wine.

8

LAMBRUSCO, SANGIOVESE, AND MORE

Lambrusco

Any discussion of Lambrusco, perhaps Emilia Romagna's most well-known wine, starts with a discussion of sparkling wine. Many wine drinkers are firm believers that Champagne and sparkling wine should not be reserved merely for special occasions. Often times, wine aficionados will drink bubbles merely because it is a Tuesday, and they believe others should do the same.

But, to understand why this is a rule to live by, it's important to understand the concept of Champagne, and of sparkling wine. With a firm understanding of sparkling wine, an appreciation for Lambrusco will follow.

What is Sparkling Wine?

Not all bubbling wines are created equal. Champagne is a term reserved for sparkling wine that is produced in the Champagne region of France. End stop. If someone is making sparkling wine in Italy, or Spain, or Portugal, or in the U.S., it, legally, cannot be called Champagne. It must be called sparkling wine. This is true even of sparkling wines made throughout France, but not within the vicinity of Champagne.

One type of well-known Italian sparkling wine is produced under the Prosecco appellation. The most common sparkling wine in Spain is Cava. There are a few grapes that are grown within Emilia Romagna that are used to produce sparkling wine. The most popular of these grapes is Lambrusco.

But there is more to sparkling wine than merely understanding where the wine is produced. At a very simple level, all wines undergo a fermentation process that turns grape juice into wine.

A sparkling wine, however, goes through two fermentation processes. The first turns the grapes into wine; the second adds the bubbles. It's possible to do this second fermentation in large tanks. The alternative is to complete the second fermentation in the bottle. The latter is a more delicate process and produces a more sophisticated wine. Wine producers in Champagne perfected this classical method in the late 1800s. It is referred to as the *méthode champenoise*. In Italy, the more traditional method of second fermentation in the bottle is called the *metodo classico*.

When purchasing a bottle of wine in Italy it is important to understand metodo classico and what it means. It is the difference between buying a simple bottle of wine, and being part of a wine Renaissance.

When our server at Agriturismo Le Casette started to pour a bottle of their house wine for our dinner, Eric and I were mesmerized. Out of the darkened bottle was a sparkling red wine, so deep in color that the bubbles themselves were purple. We took a sip. Immediately, the bubbles tickled my nose. The wine was a bit fruity, but not sweet. It was refreshing. I was hooked. We looked at the bottle and read a single word that would change our understanding of Italian wine: "Lambrusco."

During that first trip around Modena, we drank as much Lambrusco as we could. A bottle of wine with lunch, a bottle with dinner, maybe a second after dinner. When we dined at restaurants without Lambrusco, or a restaurant owner offered us something else, we begrudgingly agreed. I was fascinated with the concept of a red sparkling wine that was this deep in color, entirely different from a sparkling rose. A wine that cut through the fattiness of the cured meats, cheese, and cream sauces of this part of Italy.

During a brief trip to Modena a year later, I started to fall out of love with Lambrusco. It was the summer holiday season and most of the better restaurants were closed. We ate predominantly at the few touristy restaurants that exist in Modena, with not-so-great wine selections. Most of the Lambrusco was too sweet for my palate, and I was questioning why I enjoyed it so much during our first visit.

This changed, though, during another trip, when we visited Cantina Puianello in Reggio Emilia for a Lambrusco tasting. Not only did Giulio introduce us to the Salamino and Montericco varieties of Lambrusco, but also offered us a taste of Grasparossa. They were of a much higher quality, even though they still only sell for around 5 Euros within Italy.

My love affair was rekindled. Once again I felt confident proclaiming, "Lambrusco runs through my veins."

What is Lambrusco?

Lambrusco is a wine made from an ancient grape that is seeing a Renaissance of sorts. There are many varieties of Lambrusco produced, some of which can taste similar to Champagne to an untrained palette; some of them are entirely different. It makes

Lambrusco exploration in Emilia Romagna that much more interesting.

Lambrusco is a wine that many people are wholly unfamiliar with, depending on their age. For Generation X, who likely came to drinking age in the 1990s, Lambrusco was unheard of. The Italian wine world had been conquered by Pinot Grigio. This generation was too young to really remember Lambrusco the first time it was popular in the U.S.

With more seasoned wine drinkers in the market, winemakers have an uphill battle as they try to rehabilitate the name of Lambrusco. Apparently, in the 1970s and early 1980s, it was marketed to the disco crowd as red or pink Champagne. It was cheap. It was bubbly. It was trendy. How did an ancient grape, known during Roman times, become the mass marketed, candy-sweet Lambrusco sold to the disco dancing masses?

Drinking Lambrusco in Emilia Romagna

There are several varieties of Lambrusco, depending on the type of grape and the region where it is grown. Most widely produced in the hills surrounding Modena, it also grows in nearby Reggio Emilia and even in Parma and Lombardy. There are four DOC varietals, including Lambrusco Grasparossa di Castelvetro, Lambrusco di Sorbara, Lambrusco Salamino di Santa Croce, and Lambrusco di Modena. Although the DOC wines all bear the name of the grape, it is not uncommon for the relevant grape to be cultivated alongside other grapes.

There is a consortium whose responsibility it is to preserve the quality and promote the marketing of Lambrusco. In this case, two consortia work together, the Consorzio Tutela del Lambrusco di Modena and the Consorzio Marchio Storico dei Lambruschi Modenesi. The latter consortium focuses on the historical brand of Lambrusco.

Lambrusco Grasparossa di Castelvetro is produced only in Castelvetro, a hilly area south of Modena. The wine is sometimes referred to as the Lambrusco of the hills, and is rarely found in the flat Modena plains. In addition to producing a brilliant red grape, in the autumn both the leaves and the stalk of the vine turn red.

The Grasparossa tends to be the fullest, and darkest, embodiment of Lambrusco. This is the deep red wine that is most characteristic of Lambrusco. It can be both sweet, semi-sweet, or dry (*secco*). It is often harvested late because it tends to stand up well to the weather.

Traditionally, Lambrusco Grasparossa was a drier grape, often cloned with Barbera, which provided an acidity to the ultimate wine. During the darker years of production, including the 1970s, there was a recipe, of sorts: In order to mass-produce and mass-market Lambrusco it was made sweeter, and its traditional characteristics were overshadowed by what would sell to the disco crowd. Many of the Lambrusco producers are attempting to restore the classical characteristics of the Grasparossa, though the export market continues to be dominated by the more sweet varieties.

It is thought that Lambrusco di Sorbara was a wild grape variety, which was ultimately domesticated and probably bears little resemblance to that original wild grape. In direct contrast to Grasparossa, the Lambrusco of the hills, Sorbara grows in the plains of Modena. Specifically, on the river bed that lies between two rivers north of Modena: the Secchia and the Panaro, near Bomporto. The Sorbara grape is often grown in conjunction with Lambrusco Salamino, which is used to pollinate the Sorbara grape.

Lambrusco di Sorbara is more pink in color, rather than the deep red of the Grasparossa, and is more fragrant on the nose. Even the froth of the bubbles is tinged in pink hues. It is the lightest of the Lambrusco wines. The Sorbara wines tend to produce elements of violets, rose, cherry, and blueberry. It is considered more delicate than its cousins, making it a very easy wine to drink.

Lambrusco Salamino di Santa Croce is produced northwest of Modena, in the area around Carpi, as well as in the Reggio Emilia area of Emilia Romagna. The Salamino grape is so called because the grape bunches resemble small salamis. Despite its nomenclature, Lambrusco Salamino is sometimes thought to be the most elegant of the Lambruschi. Similar to the Grasparossa, the wine also has a deep ruby color, and a dark froth when poured.

It is possible to buy a decent bottle of Lambrusco for as little as €5. This is one benefit of drinking wine in Italy, where wines are found at a much better value than in the U.S. It's also possible to find a wine for as little as €3, but there is quite a difference in quality just within this price range. So splurge and pay the extra €2.

Some winemakers are trying to change the perception of Lambrusco, by making it seem more upscale. Traditionally, Lambrusco is made by fermenting the wine in big metal tanks until it sparkles. A few winemakers in Emilia Romagna, though, are starting to make fantastic Lambrusco with the traditional Champagne method, or metodo classico. These wines, produced metodo classico, are sometimes not even red in color like normal Lambrusco. Instead, they look more like Champagne. Although Lambrusco metodo classico is priced higher than other versions, it is a great value in comparison to Champagne.

When it comes to Lambrusco in Emilia Romagna, there is one rule on how to drink this classic Italian wine: drink it often. Generally, it is an easy wine to drink, with little complexity. It goes well with most meals and also makes a happy drinking wine. It is very easy to find in and around Modena in Emilia Romagna, but more difficult to find east towards Romagna and Bologna, where Sangiovese and Pignoletto are more popular.

Sangiovese

When people think Italian red wine, they are often thinking of Chianti, a Tuscan wine. What some may not realize is that

Chianti is produced with the Sangiovese grape. Sangiovese is the most common grape variety grown in Italy. Though people may not think of traveling to Emilia Romagna for wine, it has red wines similar to Tuscany, often at a much better value.

When looking at the wines of Emilia Romagna, there is a split in geography. There are the wines of Emilia, and the wines of Romagna. Although there are several wines produced in Romagna, including Albana, Trebbiano, and others, for a Romagnolo, wine often begins and ends with Sangiovese.

Looking at Italy as a whole, the Sangiovese grapes are used to make some of the most famous Italian wines, including Brunello di Montalcino. And, although the Sangiovese Romagna might not be able to compete in an international market with the Brunellos, the growth and increase in quality over the last decade or so has been remarkable.

There are 12 areas within Romagna that are included in the DOC specification for the region. Similar to the difference between Prosciutto di Parma and Prosciutto di Modena, the terroir of the sub-areas within Romagna can affect the quality and taste characteristics of the grapes, and therefore, the wine that's produced. To a layman, the differences, though, might be indistinguishable.

When looking at wine lists within Romagna, look for the DOC classifications of Romagna Sangiovese, Romagna Sangiovese Superiore, Sangiovese Novello, or Sangiovese Riserva. For each of these controlled appellations, the wine must be produced from grapes predominantly grown on vineyards within the winery. For example, for Romagna Sangiovese DOC, the wine can be produced by blending with other grapes. At least 85% of the grapes used must be Romagna Sangiovese grapes, but the other 15% can be made up of other grapes produced in the vicinity of Emilia Romagna.

To an untrained eye, each of the Romagna Sangiovese wines might seem similar. Each are ruby red, or garnet in color, sometimes with a purple rim. Each of them will pair well with the hearty Romagna dishes, including pasta with meat sauce, or roast or grilled meats. But, some of the Sangiovese grapes are grown on hillsides, are lighter in color, and might pair better with the fish dishes served along the Adriatic.

There is more to the wines of Emilia Romagna, though, than just Lambrusco and Sangiovese. And most of the other wines are relatively unheard of outside of Emilia Romagna. They make such finds for the wine tourist.

Pignoletto

It is true that there is more to Italian sparkling wines than Prosecco, and even Lambrusco. The Colli Bolognesi, or Bologna Hills, produce some amazing wines, all within a short drive from Bologna. The region includes the towns and villages of Casalecchio di Reno, Sasso Marconi, Savigno, Monteveglio, and Bazzano. Monte San Pietro rises about 450 meters (almost 1500 feet) above sea level, and the surrounding hills produce a unique terrain and microclimate: a climate that is perfect, it turns out, for growing grapes.

Within this region are three controlled wine appellations, including Colli Bolognesi DOC Sottozona Bologna, Colli Bolognesi DOC, and Colli Bolognesi Classico Pignoletto DOCG. Three DOC wines fall within the Sottozona Bologna, or sub zone, including the *bianco*, *rosso*, and *spumante*. The bianco is generally made from Sauvignon Blanc, Riesling, Pignoletto, or Chardonnay. The rosso is normally made from Merlot, Cabernet Sauvignon, and Barbera. The spumante is sparkling wine made in the classical method, from a blend of Chardonnay, Pinot Bianco, Sauvignon Blanc, and Riesling.

In addition to these three wines, the Colli Bolognesi DOC

includes approximately 30 more certified wines. Many of these wines are good, but they are produced with the same grapes that are known around the world – Cabernet, Chardonnay, Barbera, etc. When traveling to Emilia Romagna for wine, the real fun comes from tracking down those wines that are unique and special. Pignoletto is one of those wines.

The real history of wine growing in the Bologna Hills centers on Pignoletto, a wine first mentioned in the 1st century B.C. as "Pino Lieto." Pignoletto is an "autochthonous" grape, meaning that it grows exclusively, or almost exclusively, in one region. It is indigenous to that region. For example, Cabernet is grown everywhere. Pignoletto only grows in the hills of Bologna, and has been since its first mention during the 1st century B.C. That alone is kind of cool.

The Pignoletto grape is used to make white wines, both sparkling and still. Some consider Pignoletto to be the King of Wines in the Bologna Hills, perhaps a designation resulting from a large fish in a small pond syndrome, but well worth it. Although Pignoletto is produced across the region south and west of Bologna, the heart of Pignoletto production is in the tiny village named "Pignoletto." It sounds just as it is spelled, and easily rolls off the tongue with an Italian pronunciation (try it!). The village didn't exist until relatively recently when they realized they needed to create a place called Pignoletto to be able to give the wine a DOCG designation. And with that, Pignoletto was born.

The small village is actually set inside an Italian national park, the Parco Regionale Abbazia di Monteveglio. It's possible that the word "village" might not even be appropriate. Instead, Pignoletto is a hilltop, with some winding roads, and a handful of wineries and agriturismi.

One would anticipate that every bottle of Pignoletto produced would be similar to every other, considering much of it comes from the same locale, with a similar terroir, in this small geographic footprint known as Pignoletto. But not only does Pignoletto differ from Champagne and Prosecco, much of the Pignoletto produced differs from other Pignoletto. What accounts for these differences? They result from how the wine was made, in addition to its terrior. Is it blended with Chardonnay? Is it produced metodo classico?

Typically, Pignoletto is a delicate wine, with a light, pale yellow coloring and a crisp flavor. It is what can be referred to as a happy wine, easy to drink, less complex. It is perfect for an aperitivo, or can be served with crostini with mortadella. It also pairs well with tortellini in brodo, along with fish or shellfish.

Pignoletto can be produced still or sparkling. The still variety is generally served young, similar to Sauvignon Blanc. But it is also possible to find an aged Pignoletto, which is a way more complex wine. Aged Pignoletto is much darker in color, with a creamy taste, more similar to an aged Chardonnay. For the sparkling variety, many winemakers are producing Pignoletto metodo classico, which can be served young or aged. The various production and aging methods is what causes Pignoletto to vary drastically, even within the small appellation.

Remember the 30 wines that fall within the Colli Bolognesi DOC? Approximately one half of them are Pignoletto! The different classifications depend on whether the wine is still, sparkling, metodo classico, or *passito*, a sweet late harvest wine. There are also classifications for the various regions where Pignoletto is grown, including areas closer to Modena, or the hills of Imola.

The third Bologna Hills appellation is the Colli Bolognesi Classico Pignoletto, which received its DOCG classification in 2010. This makes it only the second white wine in Emilia Romagna to receive the DOCG title. To be qualified as DOCG, at least 95% of the grapes used must be Pignoletto. It is possible, therefore, to find both Pignoletto DOC and DOCG wines.

When looking at labels, particularly with Pignoletto, you might see the words *fermo*, *frizzante*, spumante, and metodo classico. Fermo translates to firm, or still. This is a non-sparkling Pignoletto. Frizzante and spumante can often be confused. These terms generally refer to the amount of pressure that is contained in the bottle of sparkling wine. Frizzante, or fizzy, is a more gently sparkling wine, whereas spumante, or sparkling, is more effervescent. Spumante is more likely to tickle the nose when you drink. A spumante can be made in the traditional method, like Champagne, or not.

When choosing a Pignoletto, think about whether you want the wine sparkling, and if so, how much sparkle you like. The best way to learn about Pignoletto while traveling in Emilia Romagna, though, is to taste each of them!

Negretto

Negretto is an ancient grape, from the Roman times. The word Negretto translates to something like dark, or black. The grape itself, and the wine it produced, was so dark it was almost black, giving it a very appropriate name. In earlier times, the grape was so hard to grow that the wine in its natural state was nearly undrinkable. As a result, it would often be used to color other wines, to make them darker. Although historically it was common to find grapes used in this way, Negretto's modern history is interesting.

Over the centuries, the Negretto grape fell out of production. But a few hearty, or some might say foolhardy, winemakers have rededicated themselves to the production, including Erioli Wines, Gradizzolo, and Tenuta Bonzara, making Negretto one of the most secret wines of Italy.

Negretto does not have a DOC or IGT classification. It is hard to find outside of Bologna, and perhaps even harder to find outside of Italy. It is truly one of Italy's most secret wines, but worth a taste while traveling in Emilia Romagna.

The first person to walk in the door was Giorgio. An Italian winemaker in his early fifties, with wild grey hair and a big smile, he walked over to us, greeted us with a "Bongiorno," and a kiss on each cheek. We met like old friends, despite the fact that we've only met each other once before, and don't share the same language. The only thing we share is our love of wine and good food. And, on this day, we we were there for Negretto.

The food started to arrive and the wine started to pour, all while Giorgio provided us his "brief" history of Negretto, with Helena, of Yummy Italy, acting as a dutiful translator. Giorgio is so passionate about wines, and in particular the wines he grows, that once you wind him up, he just keeps on going. Helena continuously had to interrupt him to translate before she was no longer able to keep the train of thought, bless her heart.

That is what I expected from our day of Negretto tasting in the Bologna Hills; I learned the history of Negretto, and was able to taste it, something few people in the world can claim to have done. But, like what frequently happens in Emilia Romagna, the day took a sudden turn.

The history lesson came from Giorgio, but Antonio, of Azienda Gradizzolo was the true host of our Negretto tasting, which quickly turned into a Pignoletto tasting. Antonio heard we were tasting Pignoletto at nearby Azienda Agricola Torricella. He could not let us leave without tasting his Pignoletto.

Antonio beckoned us to follow him into his winery. Language was no barrier as he guided us, inviting us to a back corner of the winery. In this dark corner was a large terracotta vat, an amphora. Antonio removed the lid, took a giant ladle off the wall, and began to pour us a generous taste of the dark and creamy Pignoletto amphora. This was no typical Pignoletto. It was Antonio's pet project, and one he was proud to share with us, even if we didn't speak the same language.

In the end, what I learned that day, and what I continue to learn from every winemaker we meet in Emilia Romagna, is that there is a passion for food and wine that unites us with people wherever we go. It's the sparkle in the eye as Antonio ladled the wine from the amphora. The speed with which Giorgio spoke of the history of Negretto. And, language is no barrier to sharing a great meal and fabulous wines.

Albana

Albana is another autochthonous grape from Romagna. Similar to Pignoletto, it is grown exclusively, or almost exclusively, in one region. Albana has been growing in Romagna since around 1300, and was also found near Bologna in centuries past.

Although it is certainly easier to find than Negretto, and a lot better known, it is still one of the secret wines of Italy, despite being one of the most representative wines of Romagna. It is mostly produced in the hills surrounding Forli-Cesena, Ravenna, and as far west as Bologna.

Albana can be produced in still, sparkling, late harvest, and passito versions. Often the still wines are slightly darker in color than Pignoletto. Despite its dark color, the taste is a lot more crisp and clean than the color suggests. It is often considered the white of red due to its flavor characteristics and complexities. The still version of Albana was also the first white wine in Italy to receive a DOCG classification, which is the highest classification of wines.

It is common to find various grapes in Emilia Romagna that are produced into late harvest or passito wines. Late harvest wines are made from grapes that have been left longer on the vine. Passito is also made from late harvest grapes, but are even more unique in that they are left to dry. For Albana passito, the grapes are left to dry for three months. Often times, late harvest or passito wines are sweeter, almost like a dessert wine. But, it's also possible to find them more dry as well.

Albana passito pairs perfectly with typical local cakes and sweets, including *ciambella*, a ring-shaped cake. It also goes well with Formaggio di Fossa di Sogliano DOP (the cave cheese). Some winemakers are producing Albana metodo classico as well, which are often light and crisp, and perfectly complement piadina.

Trebbiano

As widespread as Sangiovese is in Romagna, so is Trebbiano, the most popularly grown white grape variety in Emilia Romagna, and even in all of Italy. Trebbiano grapes are used to produce both still and sparkling wines. Generally with simple aromas and high alcohol content, it is also used to distill into a brandy. Although there are DOC Trebbiano wines, including Romagna Trebbiano and Colli di Imola Trebbiano, they are also predominantly used to blend with other wines.

And, based on the names, it is clear that it is grown and produced in Romagna, closer to the Adriatic. Therefore, Trebbiano is most likely served with piadina, cured meats, or with fish dishes popular along the Adriatic cost. The sparkling or semi-sparkling varieties also work well for an aperitivo.

Malvasia

Malvasia is another wine from Emilia Romagna that can be dry or sweet, sparkling or still. Traditionally, Malvasia was produced as a semi-sweet sparkling wine from a grape that dates back to ancient Greece. It arrived in Italy as a result of the Venetian trading routes between Italy and Greece. Centuries ago, the wine would be produced, at least partially, with dried grapes, which affects the sweetness of the wine. Currently, there are 35 different varieties of Malvasia in Italy. The most prevalent in Emilia Romagna is the Malvasia Aromatica di Candia.

Malvasia is the regional sparkling wine alternative in the western edges of Emilia Romagna. Whereas you find Pignoletto in Bologna, and Lambrusco in Modena, it is common to find Malvasia in the Parma hills and in Piacenza, and therefore on many restaurant menus in those areas.

The sweeter varieties of Malvasia are probably the most notable and most complex. Malvasia holds up quite well with the rich foods of Emilia Romagna, but the sweet versions of Malvasia, and the Malvasia passito, pair perfectly with desserts, cream cakes, and fruit tarts. Most notably, Malvasia pairs with ciambella, the ring-shaped cake popular in Piacenza. Made with flour, potato flour, eggs, grated lemon peel, butter, milk, sugar, and vanilla,

Ciambella is found in bakeries and pastry shops, and is sprinkled with powdered sugar on top.

Spergola

In the area surrounding Reggio Emilia, which is sandwiched between Modena and Parma, it is common to drink either Lambrusco or Malvasia. But, Spergola is a grape variety that is indigenous to Scandiano, a small town southeast of Reggio Emilia and southwest of Modena. The soil in the area is chalky and laced with clay, which results in a unique grape varietal.

The Spergola grape produces a sparkling, or semi-sparkling, white wine that is quite acidic. Some of the still wines are produced with partially dried grapes, making the resulting wines more intense, fuller bodied, and sometimes sweeter.

Throughout history, Spergola was often referenced alongside Sauvignon, and was thought to be one in the same. But a DNA test—yes a DNA test of the grapes—proved otherwise. Spergola is an entirely different grape from Sauvignon, and one that is only produced by a handful of wineries around Scandiano.

9

HOW TO TASTE
WINE IN EMILIA
ROMAGNA

When planning a wine tourism visit to Emilia Romagna, there are a few ways to taste the local wines. Looking for the names of the typical wines of the region on restaurant menus is the easiest way to start. It's possible to visit some of the more commercial producers of wine, those that have tasting rooms open to the public. There are also ways to experience the local wine with a little more personal touch, by organizing a day trip to one of the wine-producing areas within Emilia Romagna.

One thing about the winemakers in Europe, and particularly in Emilia Romagna, that seems different from winemakers in the United States, is the hospitality they exude. Part of this is due to the historically commercial nature of many of the top wine-producing regions of the United States, such as Napa, or Sonoma, or the Pacific Northwest. This is true of the wine regions in

France as well, particularly Champagne, Bordeaux, and Chateaneuf-du-Pape.

These are all regions where wine tourism is particularly advanced. Many of the wineries have tasting rooms open to the public. Those tasting rooms are often manned by staff or sales people. They may be passionate about wine and very knowledgeable about the wines they are pouring, but it is still not the same as speaking with a winemaker who spent hours upon hours, years upon years, producing a wine he is personally proud of.

This is the double-edged sword of wine tasting in Emilia Romagna. Yes, it is possible to visit larger, more commercial wineries to learn about the unique varietals. But it is also possible to visit the smaller wine producers, where Italian hospitality oozes. But to do so requires more planning, and more patience. It is a world where little English is spoken, but one where memories are created.

Yummy Italy Wine Experiences

When Helena of Yummy Italy arranges winemaker visits for her guests, it is entirely possible that they end up in a cellar, or a garage, tasting wines directly from the tank. Or the barrel. Or an amphora.

This is the difference between stopping for a public tasting at a larger, more commercial winery and arranging a more authentic experience. Helena acts as translator. More important, she acts as a facilitator of experiences. Experiences that are unlike many others.

In the end, many of Helena's tastings go a little off the rails, but in an entirely good way. It's possible to be tasting Pignoletto metodo classico, and suddenly the winemaker emerges with something entirely different, or experimental. (During a Negretto tasting, the winemaker emerged with a ten-year-old bottle of Pignoletto.) Any wine tourist who shows up with a passion for wine, and a willingness to learn, may be rewarded with something special.

Yummy Italy, and similar tour providers, are often able to open the door to culinary experiences that are not otherwise possible. They can indeed be a facilitator of experiences, offering opportunities that are just not possible if you roll up in your rental car.

Yummy Italy, Via Lavino 336, 40050, Monte San Pietro (BO). Yummy Italy's wine trails include customized wine visits to small producers throughout the region. Helena is a sommelier and fluent Italian speaker, and works with her clients to put together the perfect individual or small group trip.

(http://www.yummy-italy.com/wine-trails.html)

Alessandro looks like he could be Bradley Cooper's father, or at least older brother. The same eyes, the same smile. I mentioned this to Eric, and it made its way to Alessandro. Although he didn't know Bradley Cooper, we searched Google Images, and that he is normally on the list of the sexiest men alive. That certainly broke the ice. Sometimes it is necessary to break the ice with a small wine producer. Certainly it is the case when we do not speak the same language.

From that point on, we were great friends, even if his wife was a less trusting of me due to the Bradley Cooper reference. Alessandro started talking about the next time we visit. He opened bottles of rare wine, one of which was a 2008 Barbera Spumante, produced metodo classico, aged over 80 months. He only produced 1,000 bottles, which were never sold, or even labeled. Instead, he only brings it out for friends. Apparently, now we are friends. The wine continued to be poured. Alessandro grilled fresh sausages.

Alessandro produced more rare wines, the certificates he won for two of his wines, and two award-winning bottles for us to take back with us to Bologna.

After all of the food was eaten and the wine drunk,
we each had at least seven glasses in front of us, in
various stages of emptiness. Each time we finished a
glass, Alessandro would refill it. I was trying to be
professional and not end up trashed, so I tried to
leave a little in each glass to prevent a re-pour. It was
hard to exercise self control.

Alessandro suggested we visit his cellar. Of all the
wine tours we have been on, and there have been a
lot, we've never been fortunate enough to taste the
wine directly from the tank. Alessandro was in the
process of working on his recent vintages, one of
which was scheduled to be bottled in the coming
weeks. He wanted us to taste it.

We walked around the small but very functional
cellar, with Alessandro pouring tastes from each of
the large, towering vessels. We tasted Pignoletto,
Merlot, Cabernet, and more. Between the five of us,
we only had three glasses, but that was not a
problem. We passed the glasses from one friend to
another, sticking our noses in deep to breathe in the
aroma of the fresh wines. At this point I knew. We
would be returning to visit our new friend,
Alessandro.

Enoteca Regionale Emilia Romagna

Established in the 1970s, the Enoteca Regionale is located inside
the medieval castle at the heart of Dozza. It is an association of
more than 200 members, including producers of wine, balsamic
vinegar, and distilled spirits. Their goal is to protect and promote

the local wine consortia, as well as to promote the regional wines within Italy and around the world.

The town of Dozza itself is adorable. It lies just on the border of Emilia and Romagna, making it a neutral location for a wine shop looking to promote the wines of the entire region. It is a little hill top village, with pedestrian friendly cobblestone streets. Although the village and surrounding area is known for wine, over the last four decades it has also been known for the *Muro Dipinto*, an art festival of murals created by internationally renowned artists on the walls around town. Some of the murals are decades old.

The wine shop at Enoteca Regionale offers over a thousand regional wines, all tended to by sommeliers who are experienced in the various specialty wines of Emilia Romagna. They can speak not only to the history and traditions of the various varieties, but can recommend which wines work well for aperitivo versus pasta or meat dishes. Enoteca Regionale is a great place to receive an overview of Emilia Romagna wines if there is insufficient time for proper wine tours.

Enoteca Regionale Emilia Romagna, Piazza Rocca Sforzesca, 40060, Dozza (BO). The wine shop is open six days a week, during the mornings and afternoons, but closes for lunch between 1-3:00 pm. The Enoteca is closed on Mondays. The wine bar of the Enoteca is open on Sundays from 3-6:45 pm. They often run events throughout the year to highlight the region's wines. The website also lists recommendations for suggested wine tourism itineraries for self-guided tours. (http://www.enotecaemiliaromagna.it/en)

Gavioli Wine Museum

One of the many things Italy does well is museums. Even if you are not usually the biggest museum fan, there should be one exception: wine museums.

At first sight, Gavioli Wine Museum, just outside of Modena, might seem like nothing more than a wine shop, disguised as a museum, to encourage people to purchase the Gavioli wines. This couldn't be further from the truth.

Instead of a wine shop/museum/tourist trap, the Giacobazzi family patriarch has been collecting artifacts relating to wine production for at least 50 years. From a French wine press dating from the late 18th century up to more current methods of production, the Gavioli wine museum spans over 200 years of wine making history.

Walking through the two main museum rooms, the exhibits teach the process of how wine has been made over the last few hundred years, from picking the grapes, to pressing, to fermenting the wine. Many seemingly ancient tools were used up until World War II. It was a labor intensive process, including washing the bottles one at a time, inserting corks, labeling—everything completed by hand.

The Gavioli Wine Museum collection includes artifacts from Italy and all over Europe. Many of the pieces included the names of companies from nearby towns within Emilia Romagna. Some of them even included telephone numbers, the strangest of which was telephone number "92." It was the 92nd phone number that had been issued at the time.

The most interesting piece of wine history, though, includes a machine that could make any bottle of wine sparkling. It is explained like this: If there is a customer in the restaurant who wants a bottle of sparkling wine, but there aren't any on hand, then this ancient machine would make it sparkling. It is probably similar to the machines people have in their houses now that make sparkling water and flavored soda, except it was for wine!

In addition to the wine museum, Gavioli offers a transportation museum. The museum floor contains only a fraction of the collection of the Giacobazzi family. Their collection includes some Ferrari models, of course, as the home of Ferrari is only a few kilometers away. One Ferrari model was created for the American market in the 1970s and included air conditioning, a novelty at the time.

Gavioli Wine Museum and Shop, Via Provinciale Ovest, 55, Nonantola (MO). The Gavioli Wine Museum is open seven days a week, from 10:00 am-7:00 pm for tasting and selling of Lambrusco and other typical products of the region. It is better to contact them ahead of time to arrange tours of the museum and winery. (http://www.gaviolivini.com/?lang=en)

Recommended Wine Producers in Emilia Romagna

Many of the wine producers around the region specialize, or are known for, particular grapes. A winery outside of Modena will specialize in Lambrusco, or in the Bologna Hills, Pignoletto. In Romagna, it would be Sangiovese or Albana. But often times, these producers will produce a variety of wines. It is therefore difficult to make a list of wine producers based on varietals. These recommended wineries are organized based on region, along with recommendations for particular wines to seek out.

The largest of the wine producers are the ones most likely to offer tours with English language employees. Most smaller producers, though, require a culinary tour operator to arrange a visit. But, the extra effort is worth it. Even if it is not possible to visit these wineries due to distance or scheduling or lack of English, these smaller producers are the ones that should be sought out on a restaurant menu when dining in Emilia Romagna.

Wine Producers in and Around Bologna

One of the best parts of exploring wine in the Bologna Hills is experiencing Pignoletto. Although there is a sign on the side of the winding road welcoming drivers into Pignoletto, it is not a town from a political perspective. Therefore, even if the wineries are located in the Pignoletto appellation, they are physically located in the towns of Monteveglio or Savigno.

Corte d'Aibo

Following a winding road through the hills south of Bologna, this organic and biodynamic vineyard hosts a series of buildings, including an old farmhouse that has been turned into an agriturismo, complete with guest rooms. The property overlooks vineyards, wheat fields, and fruit trees. It is within this idyllic vineyard setting that Antonio, the master behind the Corte d'Aibo organic winery, produces one of the earliest organic wines in Emilia Romagna. He is also producing wines in an amphora, a terracotta vat. In addition to the Pignoletto Frizzante, a very typical interpretation of the region's Pignoletto, Corte d'Aibo is making biodynamic red wines including an Orfeo reserve, a Cabernet aged three years in oak barrels, and a Merriggio Biologico (a biological blended red), aged in the terracotta vats. Corte d'Aibo, Via Marzatore, 15, 40050 Monteveglio (BO). (http://www.cortedaibo.it/en/index.html)

Azienda Vinicola Gradizzolo

It is not easy to find Gradizzolo. Drive down the Invernata road from Pignoletto. When you think you can't go any further, keep on going. Or, come up to Invernata from the Monteveglio side. It's not simple, but it's worth the visit. Gradizzolo produces a fine 100% Pignoletto Metodo Classico. Similar to Corte d'Aibo, Antonio is also producing Pignoletto in an amphora. This version is entirely different from the young, crisp, light Pignoletto that is traditionally produced in the Bologna Hills. Instead, it is dark and creamy. Antonio is the first to admit he is not producing his Pignoletto amphora for the masses. He produces it because he himself likes it. That's passion. Azienda

Vinicola Gradizzolo, Via Invernata 2, Monteveglio (BO). (http://www.gradizzolo.it/)

Erioli Vini

Giorgi Erioli is a bit of a legend in the Bologna Hills wine-making world, and is sometimes referred to as a poet of wine. Erioli specializes in Pignoletto, and is also one of the few producers of Negretto. Although his website is in Italian, and it is not possible to visit his winery, Erioli Wines should be on the top of the list of wines to try at restaurants in and around Bologna. Erioli Vini, Strada Provinciale, Valsamoggia (BO). (http://www.eriolivini.it/)

Azienda Agricola Torricella

One of the challenging things about tracking down some of the most unique wine experiences in Italy is the fact that it can be, well, challenging. Alessandro, an independent winemaker, offers fabulous Bologna Hills wines, and unique tasting experiences at his home just outside of Savigno. It is the type of experience that is memory making, but he has no website (it's coming!) and does not speak English. Still, even with these challenges, it is worth it to use a culinary experience company to track him down. If that is not possible, search for his Pignoletto and Barbera on restaurant menus around Bologna. He bottles under the name Mastro Sasso. Via Samoggia, 534, 40060 Savigno (BO).

Wine Producers in and Around Modena

Wine tourism in the area surrounding Modena is all about Lambrusco. Although other grapes are grown and other wines produced, this is an opportunity to learn about the different types of Lambrusco.

Cantina della Volta

Christian at Cantina della Volta has a reputation in Emilia Romagna, and increasingly around the world, as being one of the top producers of high quality Lambrusco, including metodo classico. Located just north of Modena, the geography where the majority of Christian's Lambrusco grapes are grown is very similar to the Champagne region.

Christian is incorporating high-tech elements in his production process. He returns to Champagne at least once a year to continue studying how to make Champagne. He is using fancy grape presses that are computerized and controlled by someone in France. He has a technologically advanced bottling system to ensure high quality Metodo Classico Lambrusco. He is even using drones to monitor the growing process, to figure out precisely when grapes need to be picked, and to keep them safe from insects and disease!

Look for Cantina della Volta's award-winning Lambrusco di Modena Spumante DOC Metodo Classico, a red, dry, crisp, and simply perfect version of Lambrusco. There is also a rose version that is equally tasty, while being more light and fun. Their Lambrusco di Sorbara DOC Rimosso is a red, semi-sparkling wine with a second fermentation in the bottle. The Il Mattaglio Metodo Classico is a Blanc de Blanc, meaning a white wine made from a white grape (in this case, Chardonnay).

Cantina della Volta's tasting room and wine shop is open Monday through Saturday in the morning and again in the afternoon, but is closed during lunch. Cantina della Volta, Via per Modena, 82, 41030, Bomporto (MO). (http://www.cantinadellavolta.com/)

Gavioli Wine Museum and Shop

Gavioli is a larger Lambrusco producer that has a fabulous wine museum, and offers tastings and tours, seven days a week. Try the Lambrusco di Sorbara, a dry, sparkling rose, and the deep red Lambrusco Grasparossa di Castelvetro, which is common throughout Emilia Romagna. They also offer Lambrusco DOC Modena, a sparkling brut made in the classical method. The Gavioli Wine Museum is open seven days a week, from 10-7:00 pm for tastings and the purchase of Lambrusco and other typical products of the region. Gavioli Wine Museum and Shop, Via Provinciale Ovest, 55, Nonantola (MO).

(http://www.gaviolivini.com/?lang=en)

Garuti Vini

Garuti Vini is a fourth generation producer of Lambrusco. Its founder, Dante, opened the business in 1920. Specializing in the local Lambrusco di Sorbara, as well as other grape varieties including Trebbiano, they also produce their own aceto balsamico. Focused on production processes that do not involve herbicides or chemicals, they attempt to keep the Lambrusco tradition alive.

Garuti also operates an agriturismo, with rooms to rent, and traditional Modenese cuisine in the evenings. Located north of Modena, Garuti is open six days a week in the mornings and afternoons. Their agriturismo, just across the way, is open for dinner six days a week. The winery is closed Sundays, and the agriturismo is closed Mondays. Garuti Vini, Via per Solara, 6, 41030, Sorbara (MO). (http://garutivini.it/en/home-2/)

Cleto Chiarli

Cleto Chiarli is probably the largest, and most well known of the Lambrusco producers worldwide. If you see a bottle of Lambrusco in your local wine shop, chances are it is their Lambrusco Grasparossa. They offer a wide variety of Lambrusco, some of which are of a better quality than those they offer to the U.S. market. The winery is also set in a very impressive space. Tastings and vineyard tours are available, with an advanced reservation via email. They are open seven days a week from 10:15 am-5:15 pm. It is possible to request more specialized tastings ahead of time if you prefer something other than the very basic Lambrusco. In this case, request the Chiarli Lambrusco del Fondatore or Vignette Cialdini Grasparossa Quinto Passo. Cleto Chiarli, Via Belvedere, 4, 41014, Castelvetro di Modena (MO).

(www.chiarli.it)

Fattoria Moretto

A third generation Lambrusco winery, Fattoria Morreto focuses on the local Lambrusco Grasparossa di Castelvetro, which they produce in some interesting and unique ways. Their wine shop is open six days a week from 8:30-12:30 pm and 2-6:30 pm, and tastings and tours are available Monday through Friday from 1-7:00 pm, and on Saturday from 9-6:00 pm. They are closed Sundays. Reservations are required for winery visits. Fattoria Moretto, Via Tiberia 13/b, Castelvetro (MO).

(http://www.fattoriamoretto.it/en/home-2/)

Wine Producers in and Around Reggio Emilia

Cantina Puianello

Cantina Puianello offers a wide variety of high quality (and good value) Lambrusco from vineyards throughout Reggio Emilia. They also started to export to the United States and worked on a campaign to pair Lambrusco with southern BBQ called #RethinkBBQ. When you taste their Borgoleto Reggiano DOC Lambrusco you will understand why. The shop not only sells Lambrusco, and other wines, but also local meats, cheeses, and food products.

Cantina Puianello is open six days a week, from 8:30 am-12:30 pm, and again between 3-6:30 pm. They are closed on Sundays. It is recommended that you contact them ahead of time to confirm they are open for tasting. Ask to walk through the distribution area to see their cooperative produced wine, which is dispensed from machines that look more like gas station pumps! Cantina Puianello, Via C. Marx 19/A, 42020, Puianello di Quattro Castella (RE). (http://cantinapuianello.it/en/)

Medici Ermete

Medici Ermete is one of the oldest Lambrusco producers in Reggio Emilia. In addition to their wines, they offer balsamic vinegar tastings, by appointment, at their acetaia. Medici Ermete, Via Isacco Newton, 13/a, 42124, Gaida di Reggio Emilia (RE). (http://www.medici.it/en/)

Wine Producers in and Around Romagna

Poderi dal Nespoli

One of the largest, and therefore easiest, Romagna wineries to visit, Poderi dal Nespoli has a tasting room and runs regular tours of their winery. They are closed Mondays, open Tuesdays from 3-6:00 pm, and Wednesdays through Sundays from 9-1:00 pm and 3-6:00 pm. Be sure to try their Campodora Albana and Prugneto Sangiovese to sample the most typical wines of Romagna. Poderi dal Nespoli, Villa Rossi, 50, 47012, Nespoli (FC).

(http://www.poderidalnespoli.com/en/)

Poderi Delle Rocche

The result of a merger between three winemakers in the 1990s, Ettore, Paolo, and Roberto of Poderi Delle Rocche produce many wines typical of Romagna. Although their shop in Imola is technically in Bologna, they focus on the wines of Imola and Dozza. Set on the border of Emilia and Romagna, they are known for producing quality Albana and Sangiovese, two of the most typical Romagna wine varietals. It is necessary to call ahead to arrange a tasting at their little, rustic wine shop. They are located close to Dozza, so this makes for a great trip combined with a visit to the Enoteca Regionale. Just confirm which location you are visiting as they have a few. Poderi Delle Rocche, Via Punta 37, Imola (BO).

(http://www.poderidellerocche.it/en/home.html)

Tenuta Pertinello

Located outside of Civitella di Romagna, and south of Forli. Although the Mancini family just took over the production about a decade ago, they are producing some lovely wines from old vine Sangiovese grapes. Pertinello produces three varieties, one made in steel, one made in steel and wood, and the third, a Sangiovese Reserve called Sasso. Tenuta Pertinello, Strada Arpineto, 2, Localita' Pertinello, 47010 Galeata (FC).

(http://www.tenutapertinello.it/?lang=en)

Corte San Ruffillo

Drive south from Dovadola a few kilometers and follow the sign on the left for Corte San Ruffillo. A relatively new and very small wine producer, the easiest way to taste their wines is at their restaurant, which is open for dinner Wednesday through Sunday. The wine cellar is open Friday through Sunday, starting at 6:00 pm, but it is best to contact them ahead of time as it is a small operation. If you get Luca, the winemaker, chatting about his wines, he might not stop. His passion is contagious. Corte San Ruffillo, Via San Ruffillo 1, 47013, Dovadola (FC). (http://www.cortesanruffillo.it/en/)

Branchini 1858

A family-owned winery, the Branchini brothers and their family have been producing wine, and in particular Albana, since 1858. Their Albana is unique because their vineyards are located at the confluence of three rivers, the rivers that separate Romagna from Emilia. It is possible to find Branchini at wine shops in the United States as well. The Branchini winery is located just off the A14 Autostrada that runs east to the Adriatic Sea, and can be seen by vehicles passing along the highway. It is best to contact them ahead of time to arrange a visit and tasting. Branchini 1858, 4 Via Marsiglia, 40060, Dozza (BO).

(http://www.branchini1858.it/category/vini/)

PART III

HOW TO TRAVEL TO EMILIA ROMAGNA FOR FOOD

Thus far, this guide has focused on the background of what to eat and drink in Emilia Romagna. Although the first two parts contain some information on particular places to visit to taste meats, cheeses, and wines, this part of the culinary travel guide is a lot more specific. It is the practical guide on how to visit Emilia Romagna, including what cities and towns to visit, where to stay, what markets to explore, dining tips, and finally where to eat in Emilia Romagna.

10

CITIES AND
TOWNS

There are nine distinct geographic areas, or provinces, within Emilia Romagna, with Bologna at the core. The nine geographic areas from west to east include the five of Emilia: Piacenza, Parma, Reggio Emilia, Modena, and Bologna. Along the Adriatic Sea, from north to south, the remaining geographic areas within Romagna include: Ferrara, Ravenna, Forli-Cesena, and Rimini. Addresses within Emilia Romagna always include the abbreviation for the province where it is located: Piacenza (PC), Parma (PR), Reggio Emilia (RE), Modena (MO), Bologna (BO), Ferrara (FE), Ravenna (RA), Forli-Cesena (FC), and Rimini (RN).

Bologna lies at the heart of Emilia Romagna for one reason: transportation. It hosts the main international airport, and the largest train station. It's the perfect starting block for an exploration of the region. From Bologna it is possible to head north to Modena and beyond, or east into Romagna.

There are many cities and towns to explore during a culinary trip to Emilia Romagna. Many travelers will stay in the larger cities and take day trips into the countryside for their unique experiences. For others, the dream is to stay at a countryside agriturismo, or a boutique *locanda*, or inn, in a small village. There's no reason why a trip to Emilia Romagna can't include a combination of both, depending on the length of the trip.

Where to Stay in Emilia Romagna

There are a few options for accomodations when traveling in Emilia Romagna. There are a handful of Western hotel chains with locations in the larger cities, but mostly independent hotels rule. It is pretty easy to find hotel recommendations from sites like Tripadvisor. Because this is a culinary travel guide, the focus here is not on providing a detailed list of hotels in each city and town. Instead, recommendations will focus on smaller, boutique hotels and agriturismi, particularly ones that provide great food experiences.

Hotels in Italy tend to be housed in older buildings. They might include small rooms, strange layouts, steep staircases, and slightly less than functional bathrooms. The WiFi can be problematic at best. For some, finding a simple hotel to lay their head is sufficient; after all, a trip to Emilia Romagna is to eat. But, for others, a boutique hotel or agriturismo can add to the overall experience of traveling in Italy.

What is an agriturismo? Many travelers to Italy don't know about this unique accommodation option. It sounds rural. It sounds agricultural. Do you have to work on a farm to stay there? The word "agriturismo" is broadly defined as a farm stay, or any type of restaurant or accommodation that is offered on a working farm. It is essentially a blending of the words agricultural and tourism in Italian.

Agrotourism is a way for people to experience rural Italy, be close to nature, eat locally grown food, and understand where their food is coming from. It is also a great way to try something new, even if you generally tend to stay in cities and towns. And, no, it is not necessary to roll up the sleeves, put on the work boots, and work the farm.

Part of the experience of staying at an agriturismo is dining at the farm, trying dishes prepared with fresh produce, right from its doorstep. Some agriturismi will only offer meals to their overnight guests, and some are open to the public. Some offer menus, others just start bringing you food for a set price. They all focus on local specialties well known in Emilia Romagna, and generally within the province where they are located.

Some agriturismo operations are small, simple, and family run. Some are like luxury resorts. Even at a more luxurious agriturismo, there are some downsides to staying outside of the towns. It's rural Italy. It's quiet. You must have a rental car to get around. There may not be wifi. And it's possible that staff might not speak English. Because they are often family owned and operated, although everyone is friendly, it might feel a little isolated. No reception, no concierge. You may be in bed by 10 pm. For some, this sounds like a dream!

If you are looking to get away from it all, to be remote, to be in the country, you should definitely try an agriturismo in Italy. A perfect trip through Emilia Romagna should include at least one or two nights at an agriturismo, as an alternative to being in one of the cities. Even if an overnight stay is not possible, find a lovely agriturismo for lunch. There's something romantic about an afternoon meal in the Italian countryside, where it's entirely possible for lunch to stretch until 4 or 5 pm.

The Via Emilia

While traveling around Emilia Romagna one phrase continues to be uttered to describe the provinces and dining experiences on offer: The Via Emilia. (http://www.visitviaemilia.it/) The Via

Emilia is a food and wine route that runs from the Adriatic Coast on the east, west to the Po River. It runs the entire stretch of the region and includes some of the most well-known foodie areas of Italy. Although referenced in many modern marketing materials, the history of the Via Emilia dates to Roman times.

The Romans arrived in this part of Italy centuries ago. Construction of the road is thought to have started around 187 B.C. Named for the original Roman road that traversed the region, the Via Emilia and the surrounding areas are home to some of the most amazing DOP and IGP products and speciality ingredients Italy has to offer. The best part is that all of the towns along the trail are less than 20 kilometers, or about 12 miles, away from each other. That means it is easy to do a full food-focused road trip in a short amount of time.

The primary urban areas of Emilia Romagna generally are located somewhere along the ancient Roman road. Although the old Roman road has not survived, it is possible to see some remnants of it in small towns along the route. What has survived is a stretch of land that is united behind a common food tradition.

Bologna and The Bologna Hills

Bologna is the capital of Emilia Romagna. A larger city, centrally located, with the most connected international airport and largest train station, it could be considered the center of Emilia Romagna. But, more than a transportation hub, Bologna is known for its food.

Pellegrino Artusi, the father of the national cuisine of Italy supposedly said "When you hear speak of Bologna cuisine make a bow, for it deserves it." The food of Bologna is known throughout the world—from tagliatelle, to ragù, to mortadella.

The downside of this fame is that Bologna is one of the more touristy cities within Emilia Romagna. It is easier to find a bad meal in Bologna than any other town in the region. It is, of course, not as touristy as Rome, Venice, or Florence. Whereas it is possible to find a good meal on a main square in many towns within Emilia Romagna, in Bologna it is necessary to dig a little deeper.

In addition to its food history, Bologna is also known for its culture and tradition. Characteristic porticos cover the sidewalks and walkways of much of the city. Bologna is home to over 25 miles of covered walkways, and the longest single arcade in the world, which stretches approximately two miles. There are numerous medieval towers that continue to stand throughout the city, some of which appear to defy gravity. Two of the most famous towers are the Asinelli and Garisenda, the latter of which was mentioned in Dante's "Inferno."

In the center of the old Roman city is the Piazza Maggiore. It is connected to the Piazza Nettuno (which indeed offers a statute of Neptune), and Palazzo Re Enzo. In the center of these three squares is the Bologna tourism office for easy reference. Throughout the year this area fills with people walking around the pedestrian friendly city center. In the summer, chairs are set out and classic films are shown on a big screen.

On one end of the Piazza Maggiore is the Basilica of San Petronino, an architecturally unique church with a facade completed in two different time periods and in two different architectural styles, making it look almost unfinished. At dusk, it's the perfect backdrop for a photo shoot for travelers.

Just off the Piazza Maggiore lie numerous restaurants, cafes, speciality food shops, and food markets. It's easy to spend a full day wandering through the narrow streets that surround the main square.

Imola

To the east of Bologna lies Imola, often considered the eastern edge of Emilia before heading into Romagna. It is situated on the banks of the River Santerno, and is a perfect spot to stop for a meal on the way to the Romagna Riviera, along the Adriatic Sea. The historical centerpiece of Imola is the Rocca Sforzesca, a medieval fortress that is now a civic museum. From the top of the building, take in a 360 degree view over Emilia, to the Apennines.

For travelers drawn to the fast cars of Emilia Romagna, Imola offers the Circuito Enzo e Dino Ferrari. Built in the 1950s, the automobile racing track continues to welcome international sporting events.

In addition to typical pasta dishes in the region, Imola is known for many meat-based specialties. This includes mutton, and big, grilled T-bone steaks, similar to those on offer around Florence. Imola also offers travelers some direction on where and what to eat with its Wine and Flavor Route of the Imola Hills.

Bologna Hills

Heading south from Bologna are the smaller towns and villages that make up the Bologna Hills. As famous as Bologna is, the real treasures of the area lie in the Colli Bolognesi, or Bologna Hills: home to the city of truffles and wine regions that produce spectacular wines.

If you only have time for one day trip from Bologna, your best bang for your buck comes from an exploration of the wineries in these hills. It's possible to visit a couple of them in one day, with a stop at an agriturismo for lunch. In places like Napa Valley, it is possible to visit five wineries in a day, in the Bologna Hills tastings take longer and are more in depth. There's often a lot more wine poured as well. Three particular towns should be on your radar: Savigno, Monteveglio, and Bazzano.

Located about 30 kilometers, or 18 miles, from Bologna, Savigno is the City of Truffles. It is a small village, but a must-visit for lovers of food and quality food products. During the first three weeks of November, Savigno hosts its annual white truffle fair. Additionally, on every second Sunday from March to December, the town hosts a "Market of Good Things," bringing in food producers from the region. Savigno is home to one of the top restaurants in the area, Michelin Star Amerigo dal 1934. It is also a starting point for truffle hunting. Despite its popularity as a result of Amerigo, Savigno is a small town, with very few accommodation options. It is best to plan ahead.

Just down the road from Savigno, in the heart of the Samoggia Valley, is the medieval village of Monteveglio. Its historic importance was due to the location of an abbey and castle from the 11th century. The abbey continues to stand watch over the town, and is the symbol of Monteveglio. There is a festival that honors the abbey every June.

For food and wine lovers, though, Monteveglio hosts several Bologna Hills wineries, and is the headquarters of the Colli Bolognesi Wine Consortium. The tiny Pignoletto wine appellation is set inside the political district of Monteveglio. Monteveglio is also larger than Savigno, and offers more conveniences, like a supermarket.

Bazzano lies at the western border of Bologna, at the edge of Modena, and alongside the Samoggia River. Bazzano is a good place to base yourself outside of Bologna in order to visit the surrounding areas, including Vignola and Spillamberto. Bazzano is large enough to have a shopping mall and movie theaters, but also hosts the Fortress of Bentivoglio and an archaeological museum.

Bazzano is also a member of a network called the Slow Food Cities. As part of this network, Bazzano hosts one of the most important markets of the province every Saturday morning.

What to eat in Bologna

Bologna is all about meat sauce, with the most famous dish being tagliatelle al ragù. A meal that starts with a platter of mortadella rounds out the typical Bolognese dinner. Eat anything tartufo in Savigno.

Where to Stay in and Around Bologna

The Bologna Hills can be visited in a day trip from Bologna, but an overnight stay can also be a perfect city break.

Casa Bertagni in Bologna: In a sea of typical European-style hotels, Casa Bertagni stands out from the rest. A luxury guest house with a focus on art and architecture, they can also arrange unique culinary experiences within Bologna. Rooms start at €130 a night. (http://www.casabertagni.it/)

Locanda Amerigo in Savigno: Operated by Chef-Patron Bettini at Amerigo dal 1934 and located around the corner from the restaurant. Funky restoration of historic buildings, with only a few rooms available. Room rates range from €70-150 a night. (http://www.amerigo1934.it/content/show/section/locanda)

Corte d'Aibo in Monteveglio: Renovated with nature in mind, with a bio lake, freshwater pool in front. Located in the Pignoletto area. Closed over the winter months. If it's not possible to stay at Corte d'Aibo, stop in for lunch at its restaurant, and try their Pignoletto. Room rates start from €55 a night. (http://www.cortedaibo.it/en/index.html)

Casa Vallona in Monte San Pietro: A rural B&B in an old renovated farmhouse, with a focus on the countryside feeling. Their restaurant uses local, seasonal ingredients, but only serves on the weekends. Rooms start at €60 a night. (https://casavallona.com/)

Modena and the Modenese Hills and Plains

Modena is one of the holy trinity of Emilia Romagna cities, which also includes Bologna and Parma. Though Bologna lies at the center of Emilia Romagna, Modena is its heart. It is home to some of the most recognizable of the DOP and IGP products. It is the land of slow food and fast cars, being home to Ferrari, Lamborghini, and Maserati.

Modena is smaller, and therefore more manageable, than Bologna. It is easy to walk around, and it seems that all roads lead to the Duomo and the Piazza Grande at the center. At the corner of the arcade that runs along the piazza lies the tourism board to answer questions. There are plenty of cafes and outdoor dining opportunities, and the city goes crazy for gelato. But, there is one thing about Modena: everything great is outside of the town.

Yes, there are fabulous restaurants and the Mercato Albinelli, but in order to delve deep into the wines and DOP and IGP products that make Modena famous, it is necessary to escape the city. Although there are some shops in town that offer tastings of balsamic vinegar and Parmigiano Reggiano, it is more difficult to learn the details of how these Modena foods are produced if you are limited to exploring the region solely from inside the town of Modena.

Maranello

Home to the Ferrari empire and one of its museums, Maranello is a must visit for fast car enthusiasts. There are two Ferrari museums: one in Maranello, and one in Modena itself. Unless you are a total gear head, the museum in Modena might suffice. Maranello touts itself as the perfect base to explore the food products in the vicinity, though other small towns might be better suited, and have a bit more character. Ferrari tourism has almost taken over the town of Maranello.

Castelvetro di Modena

One of the reasons why Tuscany is such a tourism powerhouse are the hill-top villages. Emilia Romagna, for the most part, does not have the same sort of character. There are a few exceptions, though, and Castelvetro di Modena is one. A blink-and-you-miss-it village in the Modena Hills, Castelvetro di Modena is a great place to base yourself to explore the province. It is also home to one of the most characteristic wines of the region: Lambrusco Grasparossa Castelvetro di Modena.

Castelvetro di Modena was once a walled city, and remnants of the wall still exist. Piazza Roma lies at the center of the village, and hosts various festivals throughout the year. It is exactly what you imagine a medieval Italian village to look like. Within the village are a handful of restaurants, and Bicer Pin, a wine bar that offers tastes of regional food products. Outside of Castelvetro are a series of agriturismo, allowing you to explore more of the vicinity surrounding Modena.

Nonantola

Whereas Castelvetro di Modena is on the south side of Modena, in the Modenese hills, Nonantola is a small town, to the north of Modena, in the Modenese plains. When speaking with people around Modena, they might wonder why you would visit Nonantola at all. But, there are wineries and acetaia in the vicinity, and the Museo Lamborghini is nearby as well. There is also an adorable abbey in the center. There are only a handful of B&Bs in Nonantola, but there are some agriturismo in the area that might be another option. Otherwise, it is a good day trip from Modena.

What to eat in Modena

Where to start? Aceto balsamico drizzled over tortelloni; in the winter months tortellini in brodo; platters of Prosciutto di Modena and chunks of aged Parmigiano Reggiano served with gnocco fritto. Track down stinco, a tender pork shin, in the city center.

Where to Stay Around Modena

All of the food destinations surrounding the city of Modena are easily visited in day trips, but here are some recommendations for places to stay just in case the quiet of the countryside calls.

Le Casette in Castelvetro di Modena: Just up the hill from the town of Castelvetro di Modena, Le Casette offers simple, farmhouse style accomodations. There are dogs barking, and a handful of chickens on the property as well. The restaurant serves very good, local food, and they make their own Lambrusco. Rooms start at €60.

(http://www.lecasettemodena.com/)

Opera O2 in Castelvetro di Modena: A little further up the road from Le Casette, O2 is a luxury, modern interpretation of the agriturismo, with stunning vineyard views from the pool and contemporary restaurant. They also offer a glass-enclosed acetaia, which lines the hotel hallway. Rooms start at €100 in the low season. (http://www.opera02.it/it/index.html)

Garuti Vini in Sorbara: The Garuti family opened the first agriturismo in Sorbara. With a popular restaurant for local cuisine downstairs, an acetaia across the parking lot, and a winery on the other side of the vineyards, it is a perfect place to experience the Modena countryside. Rooms start at €70. (http://garutivini.it/en/agritourism/)

Reggio Emilia

Often an overlooked province within Emilia Romagna, Reggio Emilia has a good amount to offer. Just off the autostrada between Modena and Parma, it is a unique political region. When looking at the outlines of the city on a map, it looks like an ink splat, with tentacles reaching in every direction. Similarly, although Reggio Emilia might not have the same sort of cache as Modena or Parma, it offers tastings of some of the most typical products of the region, including Lambrusco, Parmigiano Reggiano, and even its own DOP balsamico.

The city of Reggio Emilia is referred to as *tricolore*. And, no, in this case that is not a reference to tri-colored pasta, but to the birthplace of the Italian national flag. The Piazza San Prospero in the center of town often hosts local and traditional markets, under a flying national flag.

Reggio Emilia might be a little more challenging to explore than other parts of Emilia Romagna. As much as Emilia Romagna overall is not very touristy, Reggio Emilia is probably one of the less touristy provinces within the region. Although it might be more of a challenge, there are also great opportunities to dig beneath the surface, resulting in some great experiences.

Reggio Emilia offers two unique Wine and Flavor Routes, one that runs to the south of the Via Emilia, through the hills and around a national park. The other runs to the north, leading to the Po River. When heading south from Reggio Emilia, travelers can follow the suggestions of the Strada dei Vini i dei Sapori dei Colline di Scandiano e Canossa, or the Wine and Flavor Route of the Scandiano and Canossa Mountains. It's possible to plan excursions to small towns while winding through the hills that ultimately reach the Apennines. Towns to visit include Casina, Castelnuovo ne' Monti, and Puianello.

Heading into the opposite direction is the Strada dei Vini i dei

Sapori delle Corti Reggiane, the other Wine and Flavor Route. Rather than winding through the hills, riverside towns peak out, offering a unique look at the local area, including the towns of Guastalla and Gualtieri.

What to eat in Reggio Emilia

Tricolor pasta dishes and famous desserts, including torta in cantina, in addition to Parmigiano Reggiano, of course.

Where to Stay in Reggio Emilia

Agriturismo Il Bove in Reggio Emilia: Relaxed guest house surrounded by a farm and vineyards, with some rooms having vineyard views. The restaurant offers a weekend set menu, including wine, for €30 a person. Located on the north side of the autostrada from Reggio Emilia. Rooms start at €55 a night. (www.ilbove.it)

Agriturismo La Vigna dei Peri in Quatro Castella: Set inside a 19th century farmhouse, and recently renovated, La Vigna dei Peri offers views over the vineyards, comfortable rooms, and characteristic terracotta floors. Located southwest of Reggio Emilia, closer to the hills. Rooms start at €65 a night. (http://www.agriturismolavignadeiperi.it/en/)

Agriturismo Verde Noce in Albinea: Historic, but contemporary B&B, with exposed stone walls and neutral decor. Rooms start at €65 a night. (www.verdenoce.com)

Parma

A trip to explore Parma should be less focused on the geographical differences between the towns that surround the city, and more focused on where to find food experiences. Perhaps they have their priorities right. After all, UNESCO recently named Parma a Creative City for Gastronomy.

Parma lies along the Parma River, offering riverside walks, lazy afternoons spent lounging in the Parco Ducale, or window shopping along Strada Luigi Carlo Farini. There are also churches, monasteries, and theaters to keep culture hounds busy. There is a cathedral, several beautiful piazze, and a famous pink-hued baptistery.

The city itself offers a plethora of restaurants and food shops offering up the meats and cheeses that make Parma famous. But, similar to Modena, Parma is really all about the food, and to learn about the food it is necessary to retreat to the countryside.

If time allows for only one day trip from Parma, it's usually to Langhirano, in the Parma River valley. Langhirano is saturated with producers of Prosciutto di Parma, and is home to the Prosciutto di Parma Museum. The historic Torrechiara Castle is also only a couple miles from Langhirano, making it a perfect stop for both history and historic food.

The Prosciutto di Parma Museum is just one of the Musei dei Cibo, or Museums of Food, that guide travelers to explore the towns that surround Parma. The museum's tagline is, "The history of the men and the products that have made a territory unique." Buy a card for €9 that provides entry to all of the Parma food museums and offers discounts to taste or dine in their associated restaurants. Because, if there's one reason to visit a museum, it's an opportunity to eat (or drink) at the end!

Southwest of Parma is the town of Collecchio, which is home to two of the food museums. Collecchio's history dates to medieval times, as it lies on an important pilgrim's route. It is also an important stop for a food pilgrimage as it hosts both the Pasta Museum and the Tomato Museum. The Pasta Museum starts with the flour used in pasta, then moves on to both fresh and dried pasta. As Emilia Romagna is the home to the Barilla pasta company, it can be considered an epicenter for modern pasta eating around the world. The museum houses a display on industrial pasta production, including factory machines from the mid 1800s, displays on modern techniques, and pasta advertising over time.

It is interesting to find a Tomato Museum in Emilia Romagna as it is not as popular of an ingredient in the cooking of the region, particularly in comparison to the regions in southern Italy. The museum focuses, therefore, on the history of the tomato in Italy, from its arrival to Europe from America, to its spread throughout the food culture. The final section of the museum is focused on the culture of the "Tomato World," including advertising, and of course, tomato-based recipes.

Northwest of Parma is the Parmigiano Reggiano Museum located in Soragna. The museum is set inside an old farmhouse that was in use until 1977. Currently, it displays instruments and utensils used over time to produce the King of Cheese, with some items dating from the early 1800s. The museum also addresses the importance of the Parmigiano Reggiano Consortium.

The remaining two museums lie almost directly south of Parma, along the border of Reggio Emilia. The Wine Museum of Sala Baganzola is located where wine has been produced for centuries. The museum is focused almost exclusively on the development of the wines of Parma, including the characteristics of grapes grown in the region, the history of viticulture, and historic wine-making techniques. This includes the history of barrel making, corks, and corkscrews. The museum also promotes the role of the Consortium of Wine Colli di Parma.

The last of the museums is the Felino Salami Museum, located in Felino, a small town in the Baganza valley. The town itself is characterized by its square shaped castle that dates to the 12th century, which is encircled by an actual moat.

Most of the food museums associated with the Musei dei Cibo are open on weekends, or on weekdays by appointment, from March 1 through December 8, closing for the quiet winter months. (www.museidelcibo.it)

What to eat in Parma

Almost every meal should include torta fritta, along with Prosciutto di Parma and aged Parmigiano Reggiano, followed by a plate of cappelletti.

Where to Stay in and Around Parma

Palazzo Dalla Rosa Prati in Parma: Although the decor could be considered "touristy," the location and views cannot be beat. Located across from the Duomo, many rooms have views of the cathedral. Rooms start at €90 in the low season. They also offer two and three bedroom apartments perfect for families.

(http://www.palazzodallarosaprati.it/)

Villino di Porporano in Porporano: Located only a couple of miles outside of Parma, rooms are set in a manor house surrounded by greenery and a pool. The rooms themselves are sumptuous, with hardwood floors and exposed stonework. Rooms start at €85 in the low season.

(http://www.villinodiporporano.com/en/)

Antica Corte Palla Vicina Relais in Polescine Parmenese: Famous across the region for Chef Massimo Spigaroli's culatello production, world-renowned restaurant, and 14th century wine and salami cellars. Located about 45 minutes northwest of

Parma, a 12 minute walk to the Po River, and close to the border of Lombardy. Rooms start at €200 a night.

(http://www.anticacortepallavicinarelais.com/)

Piacenza

Piacenza lies at the western edge of Emilia Romagna, bordering the region of Lombardy. It stands at a crossroads between eastern and western Italy, and at the confluence of the Po and Trebbia rivers. Located on the Bassa Piacentina, or the base of the River Po, the hillsides of Piacenza are dotted with castles. If travelers are not touring Piacenza for food, then they explore the region on so-called castle itineraries.

The location of Piacenza along the river is what gives the speciality food products of the province their distinctive taste. The Strada del Po is an 80 kilometer long route (50 miles) that winds through villages and towns filled with typical Italian porticos and piazze, as well as traditional foods.

The route runs from Caorso, through Monticelli d'Ongina, (home to a fall garlic festival), to Cortemaggiore (home to a 500 year old agricultural fair). These towns are loaded with historic fortresses and churches, dating back centuries. Even the mosaics in many of the churches honor the importance of pork to the region, often representing the ritual killing of the pig.

Piacenza is known not only for its history, but for being the "land of taste." Its food and wine not only differs from other provinces in Emilia Romagna, but also within the province itself. (It depends on whether a meal is prepared in the misty hills, or in the lowlands close to the River Po.) The biggest constant in Piacenza is the focus on salamis, including coppa, pancetta, and salame. In addition to being home to three DOP salamis, Piacenza is also home to two DOP cheeses: Grana Padano and Provolone Valpadana.

What to eat in Piacenza

Pastas including anolini and tortelli con la coda, along with pisarei e faso, dumplings made of flour and stale bread served with a bean sauce. And, of course, eat all the meat, including culatello!

Where to Stay in Piacenza

La Rondanina in Castelnouva Fogliani: One of the more upscale, contemporary options in Piacenza, La Rondanina actually lies about 40 minutes southeast of Piacenza, closer to Parma. "Like any self respecting farm, they serve only their good wines" in their restaurant. Their words. Rooms start at €80.

(http://www.larondanina.it/)

Podere Casale in Vicobarone: Set so far west that it's almost in Lombardy, Podere Casale offers a farm house with a pool. They also offer two and three room apartments, perfect for families, and a wine cellar for the adults. Rooms start at €55 a night.

(http://www.poderecasale.com/)

Agriturismo Racemus in Ziano Piacentino: A few simple rooms in a country home, a half-hour west from Piacenza. Rooms include wifi and breakfast, but plan ahead to request dinner in the restaurant. Rooms start at €50 a night.

(http://www.civardiracemus.com/)

Romagna

The Romagna side of Emilia Romagna is home to four distinct provinces, each of which has waterfront territory along the Adriatic Sea. Running south to north, Romagna includes the provinces of Rimini, Forli-Cesena, Ravenna, and Ferrara. The region can be reached by a lovely ride from Tuscany, which lies only 50 miles away.

The Romagna Riviera, or Adriatic Riviera, refers collectively to the series of seaside communities popular with Italian locals for summer sunbathing. Spanning from Comacchio in Ferrara in the north, down to Riccione in Rimini in the south, it is a distance that can be driven in less than 90 minutes. But, in that distance four provinces are traversed, and unique experiences can be had.

Many of the towns along the Adriatic are famous for promenades, gelato shops, discotheques, and mid-rise hotels and apartments that, particularly during the summer, do not offer much to tourists looking for tradition and great food.

It is possible, though, to step away from the seaside communities, or to visit in the off season, when a different view of Romagna becomes clear. Just behind the seaside towns are the mountains and hills that provide a lot of what the area offers for foodies. It is an area known for the cultivation of grapes, olives, wheat, and vegetables. It is a province of contrast: the flash of the Riviera versus the humble farmlands of the interior.

What to eat in Romagna

Pastas including anolini and tortelli con la coda, along with pisarei e faso, dumplings made of flour and stale bread served with a bean sauce. And, of course, eat all the meat, including culatello!

Rimini

Rimini lies on the south end of the Riviera Romagna, and is probably the region most characterized by Italian summer fun. Home to the city of Rimini, as well as Riccione, in the summer months bath houses, lounge chairs, and umbrellas line the beaches.

The smallest of the four Romagna provinces, its reputation is based on its waterfront activities, but the mountains stand guard behind. Due to its location from the seaside to the mountains, there is a variety of cuisines, ranging from seafood to meats. Notably, there are more oil mills in Rimini than elsewhere in Emilia Romagna.

Also due to its location on the water, the area is dotted with castles, fortresses, and forts that once offered the first line of defense against potential invasions from the sea. Instead of the hilltop villages of Tuscany, Rimini sports beautiful and historic hilltop fortresses.

It should also be noted that the Republic of San Marino sits perched on a hill, surrounded by Romagna. Located southwest of Rimini, San Marino is the oldest republic in the world and a UNESCO World Heritage Site. San Marino covers only 61 square kilometers (less than 25 square miles), but includes an impressive capital, with Mount Titano and its castle standing watch over the surrounding hillsides.

Where to Stay in Rimini

Palazzo Viviani in Montegridolfo: Lying on the border of Rimini and the Marche region, on a hilltop over looking the surrounding valleys and the Adriatic Sea. More of a boutique hotel than agriturismo, Palazzo Viviani is set inside a renovated castle. They can even help recommend a location to taste cave cheese. Rooms start at €280, so this is a splurge!

(http://www.palazzoviviani.com/)

Hotel Carducci 76 in Cattolica: Carducci 76 is located at the southern most tip of Emilia Romagna in the town of Cattolica. It provides a contemporary alternative to the larger hotels to its north in Rimini and Riccione. Its courtyard pool offers quiet respite from the busy noise of the promenade. It is only a two minute walk to the beach, with most rooms offering balconies or terraces with sea views. Rooms start at €139 in the low season.

(http://www.carducci76.it/en/)

Rex Hotel in Rimini: Located minutes from the beach, this understated hotel offers great home cooking and rents bicycles as well. Rooms start at €80 in the low season. (http://www.rexrimini.it/)

Forli-Cesena

Founded by the Romans, Forli once stood at a crossroads on the route to Tuscany. The city exemplifies both Renaissance and Romanesque architecture, and old Roman roads are still visible. Set along the Via Emilia on the way to the Adriatic, the Piazza A. Saffi at the center of Forli holds many of the city's main attractions, including the Torre Civica, or civic tower, the Palazzo Comunale, or town hall, and the Basilica of San Mercuriale, with its 12th century bell tower. On one end of the town square lies Eataly Forli, filled with local Italian food products and an upstairs restaurant with views over the square.

Only 18 kilometers (11 miles) further along the Via Emilia is Cesena, what is described as a "Malatestian town." The Malatesta family once lorded over Cesena and the surrounding areas, and references are often made to them. In Cesena, the Malatesta family is responsible for some of the most important architecture still in existence today.

Opened in 1452, the Malatestian Library is important because it was the first civic library; as such, it was operated by the commune and not the church. The Rocca Malatesta is a fortress that continues to stand guard over the old town of Cesena, similar to the Abbey of Santa Maria del Monte, visible from everywhere in town.

A group of producers located in Forli-Cesena formed the Association for the Wine and Dine Route Through The Hills of Forli-Cesena, or the Strada dei Vini e dei Sapori dei Colli di Forli e Cesena. The guide focuses on the wine cellars, farmers, and agriturismi that provide accommodations and farmhouse style meals. The guide also recommends additional towns to visit outside of the province's namesakes Forli and Cesena.

To the east, along the Adriatic is the port town of Cesenatico. Similar to its neighbors to the north, Cesenatico offers another example of Italian maritime tourism. Although the beaches can be filled with locals during the summer months, the Maritime Museum offers moored ancient sailboats. The Piazzetta delle Conserve demonstrates how fishermen traditionally stored fish in underground vats. Just south of Cesenatico, in Bellaria Igea Marina, often a large flotilla of fishing boats sail off into the Adriatic for the evening fishing run.

Several other towns within Forli-Cesena offer experiences wholly dissimilar to Cesenatico. Rather than a maritime focus, the towns on the interior focus on food production and food history. One example is Forlimpopoli.

Forlimpopoli is home to Casa Artusi, and was the birthplace of the father of the Italian national cuisine, Pellegrino Artusi. Located on the Via Emilia, between Forli and Cesena, the city is spread at the foot hills of the Apennines. Although there are many historic sites to see, the focus in Forlimpopoli is on the food. In addition to the cooking school at Casa Artusi, the Festa Artusiana is held annually at the end of June. The week-long food festival celebrates Artusi and the attempts to maintain traditional cooking techniques.

Where to Stay in Forli-Cesena

Corte San Ruffillo in Dovadola: Just south of Forli, Sara and Luca painstakingly restored a series of buildings, some dating back to the 9th century, into a stunning country resort. Contemporary rooms, with modern touches like Aroma Therapy and Color Therapy, offset the history of the collection of buildings, and the rustic nature of the surrounding farmland. Rooms start at €80, with breakfast.

(http://www.cortesanruffillo.it/)

Casa 12 in Cesenatico: A boutique hotel set on the Port of Cesenatico, with a view of the ancient boats that float out to the Adriatic. In an historic locale, Casa 12 exudes contemporary luxury. Rooms start at €100 in the low season.

(http://www.casadodici.com/?lingua=en)

Ravenna

Ravenna runs from the Adriatic Sea to the foothills of the Apennines. The city itself is known as a city of mosaics, with eight buildings on the UNESCO World Heritage List. Within Emilia Romagna, Ravenna can be considered the most historic, with ancient origins from the Romans, the Goths, and Byzantium. The city holds so much historic significance, that Dante is buried there. His tomb is located in the old city centre, the "silent area" of Ravenna. (One of the nine seaside resort areas along the coast is even called the Lido di Dante, or the beach of Dante.)

Faenza is located about 30 kilometers (18 miles) southwest from Ravenna, along the Via Emilia, and is known worldwide for one thing: ceramics. It is a city where tradition is recognized through the ceramic art that can be found in artist workshops, palazzos, and public spaces. The International Ceramics Museum opened in 1908 and hosts a selection of Faenza pottery from the Renaissance.

Brisighella is a well-preserved medieval town, set in a river valley in the Apennines. It is set in the shadow of a chalky hill with a fortress, clock tower, and a sanctuary looking over the town. The village is known for its small lanes and alleys, the most well known being donkey alley, the Via degli Asini, which was once used by chalk transporters who moved their goods using donkeys. It is an elevated covered street, with arched windows and medieval doorways. Just outside of Brisghella are thermal waters and traditional spas.

For food travelers, Brisghella is probably best known for the production of Extra Virgin Olive Oil. In the hills surrounding Brisighella, they produce some of the best DOP and IGP olive oils. It is one of the few areas of Emilia Romagna known specifically for olive oil production. Brisighella received its DOP status in 1996, the first DOP classification for olive oil in Italy.

Cervia, the city of "white gold," is the home to immense salt flats that produce a sweeter salt, considered one of the finest in Italy. The city pays homage to its ancient history, and salt wealth, by offering visitors a Salt Museum, and the Antica Pescheria, an old fish market with its original marble stands. Although no longer a working fish market, the Antica Pescheria is still stunning when hosting exhibits. Finally, the Piazzale dei Salinari, or Saltworks Piazza, houses 17th century salt warehouses. In Cervia, salt is king.

Where to Stay in Ravenna

Albergo Cappello in Ravenna: A restored 15th century Venetian-style townhouse in the old city centre. Some rooms contain Renaissance era frescoes. Rooms start at €130. (http://www.albergocappello.it/ita/)

Santa Maria Foris in Ravenna: Located in the center of Ravenna, Santa Maria Foris offers hip and chic rooms, with the possibility of breakfast on the terrace. Rooms start at €69 during the low season. (http://www.villaforis.it/en/)

Albergo La Rocca in Brisighella: Recently restored, Albergo La Rocca offers a restaurant and hotel in the center of medieval Brisighella. The restaurant's outdoor seating is located under an ancient portico, and the hotel offers a panoramic terrace with views over the village, as well as to the clock tower above. Rooms start at €80. (http://www.albergo-larocca.it/)

Ferrara

The farthest north of the Romagna provinces, Ferrara is not one of the more well-known provinces in Emilia Romagna. Home to two primary destinations for travelers, including the city of Ferrara and the village of Comacchio, the destinations are so distinct they are each worth a visit. The northeast tip of Ferrara ends with a large park set on the Po Delta, famous for wildlife and nature.

Ferrara is considered the City of Renaissance, and is a UNESCO World Heritage Site. At the center is Estense Castle, named for the Estense family, responsible for the wealth and success of Ferrara during the Renaissance. Dating from the 14th century, the castle offers a backdrop for numerous events throughout the year. Surrounding the castle are a series of Renaissance palaces, which continue to highlight Ferrara as a heritage site. The old castle walls wrap around the city, and offer a popular route for local cyclists.

Ferrara's celebrated dish is *cappellaci di zucca*, a pasta similar to a tortolloni, but filled with pumpkin. They are usually a little sweet, sometimes including *amaretti* biscuits in the recipe. Ferrara is also known for its eel as well as their "salt wines," which pair perfectly with eel. The vines actually grow in salty water.

After an evening out for pasta, it's possible to visit Al Brindisi, or "toast," which has documentation dating to 1435. This makes it the oldest wine bar in the world. Ferrara is home to food and wine events throughout the year. It is most known, though, for one of the largest balloon festivals, as well as the Palio of St. George, which offers a more historic, and less touristy alternative to the annual horse races held in Siena.

If Ferrara represents the land, Comacchio, represents the sea. Set on a cove just inside from the Adriatic, Comacchio is known as Little Venice. With historic buildings lying alongside canals, its Antica Pescheria, or Antique Fishery, still hosts a daily fish market. In addition to its historic center, Comacchio is also home to seven beaches, which start the Romagna Riviera.

Home to a vibrant fishing community, the Porto Garibaldi is one of the most commercially relevant fishing ports in Italy, and is still home to a live auction fish market. It lies only a handful of miles down the road from Comacchio, towards the Adriatic.

Where to Stay in Ferrara

Hotel Annunziata in Ferrara: Not an agriturismo, but a comfortable and contemporary hotel, located directly across from the Este Castle. You can't beat the location. Rooms start at €95 in the low season. (http://www.annunziata.it/en/)

Villa Horti della Fasanara in Ferrara: Only two kilometers from Este Castle, Villa Horti feels a lifetime away. The villa is set in a restored 9th century home, surrounded by historical hunting grounds. Rooms start at €100 in the low season. (http://www.hortidellafasanara.com/)

11

MARKETS

It's a romantic dream for travelers to Italy—wandering the local markets, purchasing fruits and vegetables. Pasta and meats. Bringing them back to your villa to create your own Italian feast.

When traveling in Emilia Romagna, there are two problems with this Italian culinary dream: First, unless you are renting an apartment, it is difficult to prepare a home cooked meal. Second, the restaurant food is so darn good!

That said, it is always fun to wander local markets in Europe, and some of those in Emilia Romagna are stunning. It's possible to pick up some fresh fruit to eat immediately, a warm pastry, prepared meals for a lunch, and even wine. Even if you are not renting an apartment, take some time to explore some of these markets.

Modena's Mercato Albinelli

It is easy to get a little intimidated by the amazing markets of Europe. Markets like La Boqueria in Barcelona receive so much tourist traffic that it can be hard to navigate. Many of the stall owners are used to travelers snaking through the narrow walkways snapping photos, but, it can get a little crazy sometimes, particularly on weekends.

On the opposite end of the spectrum, Mercato Albinell in Modena is a traditional market, which caters to the locals. It is a far cry from the touristy La Boqueria. As far as markets in Europe go, the Modena food market is not huge. It is a pretty compact space, but it holds many magical stands in its petite building. The architecture and lighting help to highlight how fresh the foods are. And, it's possible you could end up rubbing shoulders with world-famous chef Massimo Bottura.

The original Modena market was over 1,000 years old, but it was not until 1931 that the town's market was moved into its current space. The covered market is stunning, with wrought iron spirals, large columns, and even a statue of a little girl with a basket of flowers at the heart of the building. The center court statue lends an air of sophistication to the market, like they realized the building houses amazing pieces of artwork. And, by artwork, they mean food!

Along the edges are specialized stalls, with descriptive names like the Casa del Formaggi (House of Cheese). Other stalls specialize in a local speciality, horse meat, with amazing deep red hues of the flesh. Depending on the season it is possible to see (and smell) heaping baskets of fresh mushrooms of different shapes and sizes, fresh black and white truffles, and other local delicacies. A corner wine stand offers bottles of local wine for next to nothing.

The prepared foods are freshly and beautifully displayed. If you're in the mood for a picnic, pick up fresh pasta or salads, a bit of prosciutto, and other cured meats, along with some Italian cheese and bread.

The Mercato Albinelli operates Monday through Saturday from 6:30 am – 2:30 pm, and again Saturday afternoons during the winter months from 4:30 pm – 7:00 pm. The market is closed on Sundays. It is located in a smaller square, just steps from the Duomo, or main cathedral, of Modena.

(http://www.mercatoalbinelli.it/)

Bologna Markets

There are a few markets in Bologna, including traditional fresh food markets as well as ones that could be described as modern Italian food courts. There are several smaller, neighborhood food markets sprinkled throughout the city as well.

The Mercato delle Erbe in Bologna is both a testament to the history of Emilia Romagna, and the modern focus on saving food traditions. The Mercato delle Erbe, or herb market, has a history spanning more than 800 years. For almost 600 of those years, farmers and small food producers from Bologna met in the Piazza Maggiore and offered their goods to the people of Bologna.

In 1877, the city moved the market to two different locations, including Piazza San Francisco and Piazza Aldrovandi. Across the two locations, the market held approximately 450 stalls. At the start of the 20th century, Bologna realized it needed these squares for other uses. Finally, in 1910, the market moved just down the road on Via Ugo Bassi to its current location. Although the building was destroyed during World War II, it was rebuilt in 1949.

Currently, the Mercato delle Erbe hosts stalls selling fresh fruits, vegetables, meats, cheeses, and wine. It is the largest covered market in Bologna's city center, with over 60 stalls. Although smaller than the Mercato Albinelli in Modena, it is worth a visit to explore.

In 2014, the city allocated a corner of the market to host a selection of prepared food stalls called Altro? (http://www.altrobologna.com/). Altro? offers pizza, pasta, wine, and cured meats at the different stalls, with tables set in the middle. There are even a few comfy sofas to enjoy coffee or a glass of wine. There also are a handful of other restaurant stalls tucked into various corners of the market.

Although the market building is open from 7:00 am until midnight Monday through Thursday, most market stalls do not stay open that late. Instead, the building is open that late to allow entrance to the prepared food stalls at Altro?. The space is open until 2:00 am on Friday and Saturday, for that reason. It is closed on Sundays. (http://www.mercatodelleerbe.eu/#mercato)

Although the Mercato delle Erbe fits the mold of the traditional covered food markets of Europe, the old city centre offers a few additional places to shop for local food products. The Quadrilatero is the quadrilateral-shaped area of the city center lying to the east of the Piazza Maggiore. Although traditionally this space was occupied by meat, cheese, fish, and other food producers, it is now home, in part, to some luxury boutiques, including Louis Vuitton and Armani. There are a handful of food producers still located within the square.

Although this stretch of narrow alleyways is probably one of the most touristy spaces in the city, there are two interesting market-style spaces to explore. Eataly has a location running between Via Pescherie Vecchie and Via degli Orefici. They offer Italian food products for sale, and a restaurant on the top floor.

In addition, the Quadrilatero also houses the Mercato di Mezzo, or middle market. Just steps away from the Piazza Maggiore, the space has housed a market since the Middle Ages. It became the first indoor market in Bologna after the unification of Italy in the 1860s. In 2014, it was rediscovered and renovated into the current space. It is a three-story pavilion offering food stalls preparing local specialties and offering local wines. In the basement, there is an artisan beer pub.

The Mercato di Mezzo is open seven days a week from 8:30 am – midnight, making it a good alternative for Sunday exploring, when many other markets and restaurants are closed.

Emilia Romagna Shopping Tips

The Mercato Albinelli and Mercato delle Erbe offer the largest, most traveler friendly market options in Emilia Romagna. But, every city and town hosts its own local markets. There are established markets, open six days a week, in most of the larger cities. Often, the smaller towns and villages host weekly markets.

Ask at your accommodations what day the local market is. Also ask about closing times, as even the established daily markets close early some days of the week. A list of markets throughout the region can be found on the In Italy site (http://www.initaly.com/regions/erm/markets.htm). If you travel to Emilia Romagna in December, look out for the Christmas markets that dot the cityscape too.

Many of these markets, and most notably Eataly, offer amazing shopping opportunities. A word of caution for food-related souvenir shopping: Be careful what you pick up if you plan to bring products home, particularly to the United States. Items that are generally allowable include vacuum packed cheese, anything preserved or pickled, balsamic vinegar, etc. Items not allowed include meat products, some unpasteurized cheese, and possibly fresh truffles. Before dropping money on speciality or luxury food items, make sure you know what the rules are for their ultimate destination.

12

DINING TIPS

For new travelers to Italy, it might be confusing to figure out what type of restaurant to eat at. They each have different names, like *osteria* or *trattoria*. Establishments range from quick places to grab a coffee, to more formal dining establishments. So, what's what?

Bars and Cafes

Starting at the the lower end of the spectrum are bars and cafes. There are rarely noticeable differences between them as you can always order a coffee or a drink at either. It is usually possible to grab a quick snack as well. Snacks range from a pastry to a pre-made sandwich. It is common to associate bars in Italy as ones with gambling machines in them, but that is probably not the official line.

Many people will pop in for a coffee during the day, and stand at the bar. It's similar during aperitivo time, when locals belly up to the bar and chat with each other about the day's events. In many touristy areas of Italy, it will often cost more to sit at a cafe than to order at the bar. This is a distinction not often seen in Emilia Romagna. If costs are a concern, there is always a price list posted on the wall. If there is a two-part pricing system, there will be two columns of prices. The more expensive price will be the one for table service. One of the most amazing things: a *caffè*, or what Americans refer to as an espresso, will often only cost little more than €1.

There is one other type of cafe that should be mentioned, a *pasticceria*, or pastry shop. Also serving coffee, the pastry shops offer a wider variety of pastries, or fancier sandwiches. Many also will sell pastries for takeaway.

There is one other type of bar: an *enoteca*, or wine bar. Enoteca are where Italian bars start the transition to restaurants. An enoteca is a wine shop that also serves food, and a much wider selection of wines than a normal bar or cafe. It's usually possible to order platters of meats and cured cheeses, but they may also have kitchens that serve warm food.

There is one final type of cafe that does not traditionally exist in Italy outside of Emilia Romagna. It is common to find places called a *piadineria*, or *tigellerie*. These are places that focus on selling piadina or plates of tigelle. Sometimes this will include breads served with platters of meats or cheeses. Often times, the meat or cheese is served inside the sliced bread, similar to an Italian version of a sandwich. For example, it is possible to order a sampling of three or five tigelle, with different meats or cheeses inside, along with a glass of wine. They are very common for lunch crowds, or for snacks. It's possible to even find them at the shopping malls.

Restaurants

Starting on the more simple end of the scale, a *tavola calda* is a cafeteria-style restaurant. Translating to "hot table," they may offer warmed, pre-made foods all day and can be a less expensive option to more formal restaurants. One of the reasons why they're a good alternative for those on a budget is because they don't add a cover charge to the bill as they do at other restaurants.

Another less formal option is a pizzeria. Some may include sit down areas; some may serve pizza by the slice. *Pizza al taglio* is a pan pizza, normally ordered and paid for by weight. One thing to note is that pizza is not a traditional dish in Emilia Romagna. It's not as a common as in Rome or Naples, where tomatoes are much more prevalent in the cuisine. Many of the places in Modena and Bologna, for example, advertise Sicilian or Napoli style pizza. It is quite easy to spend two weeks touring Emilia Romagna without eating a single pizza.

Traditionally, the distinctions between an *osteria*, a *trattoria*, and a *ristorante* were more clear. In recent times, it's become a lot more murky.

An osteria initially was an inn, a place that offered wine along with accommodations. Imagine the scene of rowdy, older men, drinking wine that's been kept in an barrel in the back by an inn-keeper. This is certainly not the case today, but it is likely an osteria will focus more on traditional cuisine. The exception being Osteria Francescana, the farthest thing from a simple and traditional dining experience in Emilia Romagna.

A trattoria is more formal than an osteria, but less formal than a ristorante. Doesn't that just say it all? Traditionally, a trattoria was more rustic, often family-owned, and would offer house wine from a decanter. The food was simple and often changed with the seasons to focus on locally available ingredients.

It is hard to tell the difference between an osteria and a trattoria today. As both are less formal than a ristorante, they might be a good option if you are looking for a bowl of pasta and a glass of wine, and do not want a full restaurant experience.

A ristorante is definitely the more formal of the possibilities found in Emilia Romagna. Think linens, flatware, china. Servers might be more professional, or more knowledgable. There would be a host and most likely a sommelier.

Although many ristorante in Emilia Romagna may still offer traditional dishes, there's likely to be a lot more experimental or contemporary options as well. Pricing may vary, and just because the storefront says "Ristorante," it doesn't necessarily mean it's the most expensive of the options. Check the menu to be sure. One thing to note: because a ristorante is the traditional spot for a more formal meal, it's customary to order more than one course.

Other Dining Tips

With any of the above options, be sure to ask for a menu or search for a list of prices ahead of time to ensure you are not caught off guard. And, don't forget the cover charge applied at many ristorante, trattoria, and osteria. It may range from €1-3 a person and can be considered a service charge, of sorts, although technically it is the charge for the table cloth and the bread.

One of the more frustrating things about traveling through much of Europe is determining when to eat what where. Lunch is rarely eaten before 1pm. This is because unlike the three meals a day Americans are used to, many Italians eat a snack during the late morning to tide them over to lunch. Lunch is often the biggest meal of the day, particularly on the weekends when a big lunch is a family affair. And, don't be surprised to see many people, even folks on their lunch break, enjoying a glass of wine (or two) during lunch.

Dinner in Italy is not as late as dinner in Spain, but is rarely enjoyed before 8pm. It's a time to relax and enjoy the company of the people you are with. It is often also a multi-course meal. A traditional Italian dinner will include a starter, pasta course, a meat course, and a dessert. For many, this is nearly impossible to maintain over a holiday. As an alternative, it is acceptable to share a starter, particularly an antipasti plate of cured meats. The less formal the restaurant, the more acceptable it is to skip a course or two.

As for dessert, although it is customary to order a dessert, it is possible to share. It is also customary to order a coffee, generally a caffè (espresso), which will arrive after the dessert is complete.

In many more traditional osteria and trattoria, particularly in smaller towns, the owner or server may place a bottle of *nocino* on the table as an after-dinner drink. Nocino is a walnut liqueur. In addition to the hulls of walnuts, when the nuts are still green, the liqueur is infused with lemon peel, cloves, and cinnamon. If the owner or server places it on the table, there is typically no charge for a single glass for each person. If the guests start to get a little heavy handed with the bottle, a charge may appear.

A note about the tradition of Italian aperitivo: In its most literal sense, aperitivo is a drink before dinner. It is something to whet the appetite, or to hold people over until a later dinner. In much of northern Italy, including Milan, aperitivo is an institution. It is common to order a drink and receive a snack, or have available a buffet of options, including warm pasta dishes.

Although aperitivo is less popular in Emilia Romagna, it is still possible to find, most notably in Bologna or Modena. It is popular in Bologna because of the number of students in the university city. For many students, an aperitivo is a way to socialize with friends and eat cheaply. For food travelers, an evening aperitivo might be a great option after a long afternoon lunch, when there is simply no room in the belly for a full dinner.

In some cases a glass of wine or a cocktail, like an Aperol Spritz or Lambrusco Spritz, might be served with a little sandwich. In other places, a buffet is placed out, often of cured meats and cheeses. The price of the drink, often €5 or €6 a glass, will include the snacking option. If looking for an aperitivo option, just wander the streets of Bologna and peek inside the bars and cafes, looking for people having a drink at a buffet.

What's This Mean?
How to negotiate a menu in Italy.

Travelers to Emilia Romagna have often traveled to Italy before, but just in case, here's a primer on some important words to know on a menu.

Antipasti: A starter or appetizer

Primi: A pasta or risotto course

Secondi: A meat or fish

Contorni: A side dish, normally roasted potatoes or a grilled vegetable (A meat dish often will not come with a side. If your server asks if you would like a vegetable or potato, there will be an extra charge.)

Dolce: Dessert

13

WHERE TO EAT IN
EMILIA ROMAGNA

Why did it take 12 previous chapters to finally get to the list of where to eat in Emilia Romagna? Because the food culture of Emilia Romagna is so important to understand. Restaurants are only part of the experience.

With so many great food options in Emilia Romagna, it's really hard to go wrong, particularly when you explore outside of the cities like Bologna and Modena. This list of restaurants is not exhaustive. Instead, it's meant to offer some reliable options in the cities, towns, and villages where travelers are most likely to visit across the region.

As for pricing, most of these recommendations range between €7-10 for a plate of pasta and €9-15 for a meat course. Antipasti platters can range from as little as €6 for a plate of prosciutto to €15 or more for speciality meats, like culatello. It is quite easy to have a good meal for two people, including one antipasti, two pasta, one secondi, and a bottle of wine for less than €50, and all of it will be delicious. Some restaurants or agriturismi offer set menus for about €35 including wine. The few restaurants named below that are more pricy will be noted with a €€€.

Many of the websites included are not in English, and many of the restaurants themselves do not offer an English menu. This culinary travel guide hopefully provides enough guidance to suggest a handful of dishes on menus throughout the region, even if those menus are in Italian. There is no way to go hungry.

It is also important to check the websites or Facebook pages of the restaurants before you go. Many restaurants will close one or two days a week, often on Sundays, but sometimes on Mondays. Ask your hotel to call ahead. The descriptions below will include closing days, if available, as listed at the time of publication. Also, most restaurants are open for lunch and dinner, but will close during the middle of the day, often from 3pm until approximately 7pm.

In and Around Bologna

Bologna Central

Bologna is one of the few areas in Emilia Romagna where you might not find great food. It is the largest, and most touristy, of the cities and towns. As a result, if you are not careful and don't plan ahead, you might be disappointed. This is particularly true in the city center north of Piazza Maggiore, in the restaurants that flank Via dell'Indipendenza.

Trattoria Bertozzi

If looking for a typical Bolognese restaurant, away from the crowds, and the tourists, this is the place. Set outside of the city center, close to the football stadium, tiny Trattoria Bertozzi squeezes in a handful of tables. And, they are filled with reservations almost every night, despite the fact that the restaurant has no real website, no updated Facebook page, and doesn't advertise. Have the hotel call ahead for reservations. Their handmade pastas are the real draw, along with the chef's explosive personality.

Trattoria Bertozzi, Via Andrea Costa, 84/2, 40134 Bologna (BO). Reservations can be made by calling the restaurant (+39 051 614 1425).

(http://www.trattoriabertozzi.it/)

Eataly

The Bologna branch of the international chain of Italian shops and restaurants. Centrally located, Eataly is a good option for a less expensive and casual lunch. It can be a bit hard to find. Look for the bookstore just off the Piazza Maggiore and take the stairs up. It is often crowded, so be patient.

Eataly Bologna, Via degli Orefici, 19, 40124 Bologna (BO). Managed by Alberto Bertini of Trattoria Da Amerigo in Savigno, and focused on local dishes with vegetables straight from the farm. Open seven days a week. Eataly doesn't close during the afternoon, so it's a good option when most other places are closed.

(http://www.eataly.net/it_it/negozi/bologna/)

Mercato di Mezzo

Just across the pedestrian only street from Eataly is another popular, but reliable option. A Bolognese version of a food court, there are options for everyone, including a stall with local wines and artisan beers in the basement. It can get crowded, so best to try the Mercato di Mezzo outside prime eating times. The pasta shop on the corner is an option to try all different types of pasta, with various sauces. With a wine bar at the next counter over, it's also the easiest. RoManzo also offers great burgers and meats, with the meat supplied by one of Emilia's finest butchers.

Mercato di Mezzo, Via Drapperie, 40124 Bologna (BO). Similar to Eataly, Mercato di Mezzo is open all day, seven days a week.

Altro? at Mercato delle Erbe

Set inside an old market in Bologna, it's still the place to go for fruits, vegetables, and flowers during the day. On one end is a modern Bolognese interpretation of a food court, Altro?, with pasta, meats, cheeses, and wine. A little more formalized than Mercato di Mezzo, there is an option to have a sit down dinner with service. Keep walking through the far side of the market from Via Ugo Bassi in the evenings to find young people having an aperitivo outdoors.

Altro? Via Ugo Bassi, 25, Bologna (BO). The building is closed on Sundays. The food court is open all day six days a week.

(http://www.altrobologna.com/)

Osteria dell'Orsa

A popular spot for university students, and a short stroll from Piazza Maggiore. Expect traditional pasta dishes served to diners at communal tables drinking carafes of house wine.

Osteria dell'Orsa, Via Mentana, 1, 40126 Bologna (BO). Open all day, seven days a week, but closed for Christmas and New Years.

(http://www.osteriadellorsa.com/)

Antica Trattoria del Reno

This is not a restaurant that a traveler just happens upon. It is set in an industrial area, outside of the city center, close to the airport. But, the location allows Chef Vicenzo to offer experimental dishes at a more reasonable price than the rents would allow in the center of Bologna. It is not the place to experience a traditional Bolognese meal. Instead, some of the dishes translate to "Laughter of Taste" or "In the Wood." Antica Trattoria del Reno is the place to enjoy the next stage of Italian cuisine.

Antica Trattoria del Reno, Via del Traghetto, 5/3, 40100, Bologna (BO). Closed Sundays. Open for lunch and dinner Thursday, Friday, and Saturday. Open for lunch Monday, Tuesday, and Wednesday, and dinner on those days by appointment only. €€€ Starters from €10-18 and entrees from €18-22.

(http://anticatrattoriadelreno.it/)

Osteria al 15

Just a 10-minute stroll from the Piazza Maggiore, in a quiet part of town, Osteria al 15 is a "blink and you'll miss it" restaurant, that is barely recognizable from the outside. Inside, it's a little classic kitsch, with walls covered in historic memorabilia. Cheap house wine. Limited menu of traditional pastas and meats. Try the ricotta cheese with saba. Or order a sample of two or three pasta dishes all served on one plate, to let you try more.

Osteria al 15, Via Mirasole, 13, 40124 Bologna (BO). Opens at 7:30 pm for dinner only. Closed on Sundays. Reservations recommended on the weekends via their phone number (+39 051 331806) as they do not have a website or Facebook page.

Ristorante Pizzeria Jari

As much as pizza is not a traditional thing to find on menus in Emilia Romagna, sometimes you just want one when you're in Italy. There are a handful of places advertising pizza in the center of Bologna, most very touristy and of dubious quality.

But, there's a little family-run place on the other side of the train station. They offer good pizza, great pasta, and a small wine list that includes a favorite, Corte d'Aibo Pignoletto.

Ristorante Pizzeria Jari, Via Sebastiano Serlio, 2, 40128 Bologna (BO). Open for lunch and dinner Tuesday through Friday, dinner only Saturday and Sunday, and closed on Mondays.

(https://www.facebook.com/PizzeriaRistoranteJari)

Savigno

Amerigo dal 1934

If you have a thing for truffles, Savigno should be a destination on your list. It's the city of truffles. It's possible to go truffle hunting nearby. Then, dine on a truffle-filled Michelin Star menu at Amerigo, with Chef-Patron Alberto Bettini. His claim to fame is his seasonal truffle egg. A must try, but perhaps share it among the group lest you have truffle overload. Alberto also offers a great selection of local wines from the Bologna Hills. If you plan to overdo your wine consumption, Amerigo has a few rooms in a little artistic inn a few blocks away from the restaurant.

Amerigo dal 1934, Via Marconi, 14-16, 40060 Savigno (BO) Marked €€€ but really only for the truffle menu. Closed on Monday year round, and Tuesday during the winter months (January through March). Open generally for dinner only, but they offer lunch on Sunday and during festival days in Savigno.

(http://www.amerigo1934.it/)

Monteveglio

Agriturismo Gradizzolo

Set at the edge of the national park that runs through the center of Monteveglio. If you follow Google Maps through the Pignoletto region, just keep going. Eventually you will find it. One of the best young chefs in the area, Chef Chiara makes a mean ragù, a fabulous local pasta called gramigna, and some of the best pork in the Bologna Hills. If looking for a unique wine option, try the Pignoletto Anfora, aged in terracotta vats, similar to how the Romans made wine.

Agriturismo Gradizzolo, Via Invernata 2, 40050 Monteveglio Valsamoggia (BO). Open for lunch and dinner Monday through Thursday, lunch only Friday and Saturday, and dinner only on Sunday.

(http://www.gradizzolo.it/)

Corte d'Aibo

Another option in the Pignoletto region of the Bologna Hills that has some of the best pork in Italy. Corte d'Aibo is a biologic and organic farmhouse, offering agriturismo style rooms, a restaurant open to the public, and a winery. Offering a pre-set menu, which changes monthly, Corte d'Aibo specializes in traditional dishes. The menu might include pasta made with vegetables from their organic garden, followed by a stuffed guinea fowl, flavored with their own Pignoletto. If there is pig cheek or beef cheek on the menu, don't pass it up.

Corte d'Aibo, Via Marzatore, 15, 40050 Monteveglio (BO). Closed Tuesday and during the winter months.

(http://www.cortedaibo.it/)

Trattoria Dai Mugnai

In the center of Monteveglio, Dai Mugnai is set in one of the oldest buildings in Monteveglio, dating back to 1500. Mugnai translates to "the miller," in reference to the flour mill that once stood in the building. Dai Mugnai offers antipasti platters of local meats, including Culatello di Zibello, served with fresh crescentine. Their pasta menu includes all of the local favorites, including tortellini in brodo, tortelloni with aceto balsamico, and tagliatelle al ragù. Their wine list is also one of the best in the area.

Trattoria Dai Mugnai, Via Mulino 11, 40050 Monteveglio (BO). Open for lunch Tuesday through Sunday, and dinner on Tuesday, Friday, and Saturday. Closed on Monday.

(http://www.daimugnai.it/)

Castiglione dei Pepoli

Taverna Del Cacciatore

Your chances of just stumbling upon Taverna Del Cacciatore are pretty slim. Either it's a planned stop off the highway on the way to Florence, about an hour south of Bologna, or it's an afternoon trip specifically to taste the food from the reigning Queen of Tortellini in 2016. Yes, the chef is the tortellini queen, and actually wears a silver tortellini on a chain around her neck. In addition to pasta, the very rustic meat courses include a version of *porchetta*, pork stuffed with rabbit, or a risotto *colombaccio*, a common wood pigeon.

Taverna Del Cacciatore, Via Cavanicce, 8, 40035 Castiglione dei Pepoli (BO). Open for lunch and dinner Tuesday through Saturday, lunch only on Sunday (until 5:00 pm). Closed on Monday.

(https://www.facebook.com/lareginadeltortellino/)

In and Around Modena

Modena Central

Trattoria Aldina

Stinco. One word describes why a visit to Trattoria Aldina is required. Just across the pedestrian friendly road outside of the Mercato Albinelli, head upstairs into an apartment building. You almost feel like you are entering someone's house for lunch, or to a speakeasy. Focusing on typical Modenese cuisine and handmade pastas. There is no menu. The server walks up and speaks the menu, generally in Italian. If she says the word stinco, order it. A slow roasted pork shin, it's fabulous.

Trattoria Aldina, Via Luigi Albinelli, 40, 41121 Modena (MO). Closed Sunday. Open for lunch six days a week and dinner only on Friday and Saturday. Reservations recommended. Email trattoria.aldina@gmail.com.

Trattoria del Giardinetto

A little hokey, and overly decorated with pig-themed artwork, Trattoria del Giardinetto offers a large outdoor seating area (with a view over a parking lot). It seems to be a hit with groups and students, particularly for its gnocco fritto and cured meat platters. It's also pretty easy on the wallet, and a good casual alternative to more formal dining options in Modena.

Trattoria del Giardinetto, Piazzale Paolo Boschetti, 1, 41100 Modena (MO). Open Monday through Friday for lunch and dinner and dinner only on Saturday. Closed on Sunday.

Ristorante Da Enzo

A reliable option in central Modena. Known for pasta, desserts, and friendly English speaking servers. They offer a typical regional menu, and may feel a bit more touristy than other Modena restaurants, but still pleasant. If your first stop in Emilia Romagna is Modena, Da Enzo is a good option to get your feet wet with the local specialities.

Da Enzo, Via Coltellini, 17, Modena (MO). Open for lunch and dinner Tuesday through Saturday, and for lunch only on Sunday. Closed Monday.

Ristorante Da Danilo

Located almost next door to Da Enzo, Danilo is a step ahead of Da Enzo because of its authentic, local feel. Its authenticity is proven by being one of the few places offering *bollito misto*, served in steaming trays in the dining room. Bollito misto is a mixed plate of various boiled meat products, potentially including tongue, intestines, pig feet, and more. They also serve cotechino, served with lentils or beans. If you're not feeling all that adventurous, stick to the tortellini in brodo di cappone. Cappone is a castrated rooster, and it gives the broth a unique bite. Or, try the tortolloni Modenese, drizzled in balsamic vinegar.

Da Danilo, Via Coltellini, 31, 41121 Modena (MO). Open for lunch and dinner Monday through Saturday. Closed Sunday.

(http://www.ristorantedadanilomodena.it/)

Restaurante Uva d'Oro

Another reliable option in Modena. When the craving comes for pizza, this is a perfect option. They are also almost always open, even during holidays when nothing else is. In addition to a big pizza menu, they offer gnocco fritto and salumi platters. There is a large outdoor seating area overlooking a pretty square as well.

Restaurante Uva d'Oro, Piazza Giuseppe Mazzini, 38, 41121, Modena (MO). Open seven days a week for both lunch and dinner.

(http://www.ristoranteuvadoro.it/)

Plan Ahead Options

Two other options in Modena require planning ahead. Very ahead. Osteria Francescana (€€€) on Via Stella is Chef Massimo Bottura's three Michelin Star restaurant. It's expensive (think €300 a person) and contemporary, and has a wait list of at least six months. But, in 2016 it was named the number one restaurant in the world by The World's 50 Best, so perhaps it's worth it. Osteria Francescana, Via Stella, 22, 41121, Modena (MO). Don't rely on the website for reservations. Instead, the phone lines open on the first day of every month. Seats normally sell out within 10 minutes.

(http://www.osteriafrancescana.it/)

Hosteria Giusti is another option, less expensive than Osteria Francescana, and more traditional. It has an impeccable reputation, but only a handful of tables. Booking ahead is required. Hosteria Giusti, Via Farini, 75, 41100, Modena (MO). Open for lunch only Tuesday through Saturday.

(http://www.hosteriagiusti.it/lhosteria/)

Castelvetro di Modena

Opera 02

A contemporary boutique hotel, unlike anything else in the area, O2 offers fine dining, regional specialities, and a view over the Modenese hills. O2 calls itself an agriturismo, but it's modern architecture and sometimes creative cuisine tells otherwise. Open every day for both lunch and dinner, O2 is a perfect alternative to a historic trattoria or osteria. Although they continue to focus on traditional dishes, and local ingredients, there is more creativity here. Try the tagliatelle al ragù, made with beef from the famous Modenese white cow, or the tortelli stuffed with ricotta made, also, from the same type of cow, served simply with butter and sage. Of course, wash it all down with Lambrusco. They also offer a gluten-free tasting menu, surprising in Emilia Romagna.

Opera O2 Di Ca' Montanari, Via Medusia, 32, 41014 Levizzano di Castelvetro Modena (MO). Open seven days a week for both lunch and dinner.

(http://www.opera02.it/en/index.html)

Agriturismo Le Casette

Just outside of town, and before heading too far down the country road to Opera O2, is a traditional agriturismo, at the opposite end of the spectrum from O2. It's a less expensive, more casual option, offering set menus for €20. A must-try includes their fresh and warm gnocco fritto with local meats. They often keep the menu rustic, offering hare and guinea fowl. Try it!

Agrituriso Le Casette, Via Ghiarone 63, 41014, Castelvetro di Modena (MO). Open daily for lunch and dinner during the high season. During the fall and winter it is best to call ahead to ensure they will be open.

(http://www.lecasetteagriturismo.com/)

Maranello

Ristorante Montana

Most visitors to Emilia Romagna make a stop in Maranello, home to Ferrari, and the fast car tourism industry. There are a handful of cafes walking distance from the Ferrari museum, but if you have a car and can drive just five minutes down the road, there is a real treat waiting at Ristorante Montana.

Stepping into Ristorante Montana is very similar to stepping foot inside the Ferrari museum; the walls are covered with memorabilia. At first blush, the restaurant screams tourist trap. Instead, most of the diners, particularly at lunch, are local businessmen. The prices for a full dinner can get a bit pricey, but the lunch time prix-fixe is a good deal. They also offer a sampling plate of two or three pastas so you can taste some of the different traditional Emilia Romagna offerings.

Ristorante Montana, Via XX Settembre, 3, 41040 Spezzano di Fiorano (MO). Open Monday through Friday for lunch and dinner, and for dinner only on Saturday. Closed Sunday.

(http://www.ristorantemontana.it/eng/locale.htm)

Nonantola

Osteria di Rubbiara

A restaurant that falls squarely onto the list of restaurants worth driving to. Set inside one of the top acetaia in Modena, the restaurant is in a "blink and you'll miss it" town. The restaurant and acetaia are really the only commercial enterprises in this small village outside of Nonantola. There is a pre-set menu, at a fixed price. They don't even walk you through the menu; they just start bringing courses. It's a gut-busting meal, including two pastas, two meat courses, and dessert. They've been operating since the 19th century this way. They are so traditional, you must check your cell phones at the door. But it's all worth it.

Osteria di Rubbiara at Acetaia Pedroni, Via Risaia, 2, 41015 Nonantola (MO). Closed Tuesdays. Open for lunch six days a week, and on Friday and Saturday for dinner.

(http://www.acetaiapedroni.it/en/osteria/)

La Piazzetta del Gusto

An easy option in the heart of Nonantola, set on the *piccolo* town square. They also run their own pasta shop next door, where handmade pasta of all shapes and sizes is made fresh each day. They specialize in local Emilia Romagna pastas, including passatelli and garganelli as well as tortelloni vecchia Modena, with bacon, Parmigiano Reggiano, and balsamic vinegar. If you are going to try passatelli anywhere, it should be at La Piazzetta as they pride themselves on various preparations of this unique pasta.

La Piazzetta del Gusto, Via Roma, 24, 41015 Nonantola (MO). Open for lunch Tuesday through Sunday, and for dinner Tuesday through Saturday. Closed Monday.

(http://www.lapiazzettadelgusto.com/en/)

Soliera

Fattoria Maria

Also located outside of Modena, Fattoria Maria is a must-visit if heading into the outskirts of Modena. Traditional cuisine from a family owned and operated agriturismo. During nice weather sit outside on the patio, with the family dog, and a view over the fruit trees. After a Sunday lunch walk around the building and visit the chickens. Definitely order freshly sliced salumi with gnocco fritto and their handmade pasta.

Fattoria Maria, Via Stradello Lama, 157-163, 41019 Soliera (MO). Open for dinner Wednesday through Saturday, and for lunch on Sunday. Reservations recommended.

(http://www.fattoriamaria.com/)

Sorbara

Garuti Vini

The Garuti family started producing wine in Modena over a 100 years ago. Their restaurant is set inside a renovated rustic farm house, with the vineyards separating you from the winery and cantina. Be sure to order the tortelloni with their own aged aceto balsamico.

Garuti Vini, Via per Solara, 6, 41030, Sorbara (MO). The agriturismo is open for dinner Tuesday through Saturday, as well as lunch on Sunday. They are closed Monday. It's also possible to visit the winery during lunch.

(http://garutivini.it/en/home-2/)

In and Around Reggio Emilia

Ristorante Canossa

Situated in the historic center of Reggio Emilia, Ristorante Canossa is dedicated to keeping traditional cooking techniques alive. This includes fresh, handmade pasta, and bollito misto (roasted and boiled meats.)

Ristorante Canossa, Via Roma, 37, 42121 Reggio Emilia (RE). The restaurant is open for lunch and dinner six days a week. They are closed on Wednesday.

(http://www.ristorantecanossa.com/)

Osteria Della Capra

The restaurant of the goat (*capra*), specializes in Emilian cuisine, including freshly made tigelle, local salumi, desserts made in-house, and a collection of Lambrusco Reggio Emilia. One of their more unique dishes is a multi-colored pasta, where the brown colored pasta is flavored with chocolate, served in a culatello and truffle sauce. They also offer *torta in cantina*, a very, very local dessert—essentially a sweet bread soaked in liquor.

Osteria Della Capra, Via Andrea Rivasi, 34, 42025 Cavriago (RE). Tucked into a two-story pink house, which looks like it is defying gravity, just at the edges of Cavriago. Tasting menus range from €20 to €25, including wine. Open for lunch and dinner on Tuesday, Wednesday, Friday, Sunday, and Monday, but dinner only on Saturday. Closed Thursday.

(http://www.osteriadellacapra.it/)

Ristorante Cattini

Famous for their rustic cuisine, including tortelli stuffed with pumpkin or spinach. The owner of the restaurant, Cesare, passed away in 2016, at the age of 86. Prior to this, he was often found walking the bollito misto trolley around the dining room. Hopefully someone will keep up his tradition.

Ristorante Cantini, Via Filippo Re, 20, 42020, Quattro Castella (RE). Ristorante Cantini is open Tuesday, Wednesday, Thursday, and Sunday for lunch, and on Friday and Saturday for both lunch and dinner. They are closed on Monday.

(https://www.facebook.com/RistoranteCattini/)

Il Vulcanetto del Querciola

Specializing in local grilled foods, including grilled polenta and grilled Parmigiano Reggiano. They also offer somewhat unique dishes including tagliatelle in a broth and oven roasted cannelloni.

Il Vulcanetto del Querciola, Via Salone, 3, 42030 Regnano (RE). Prices start at €20 per person for the vegetarian menu. Yes, they have a vegetarian, and even a vegan, menu. The regular set menu ranges from €30 to 35 per person.

(http://www.ilvulcanettodelquerciola.it/)

In and Around Parma

Parma Central

Ristorante La Forchetta

La Forchetta, in the center of Parma, offers a fine dining atmosphere inside, and a slightly more casual atmosphere on the patio. In Parma, they take their prosciutto seriously, and sometimes offer various ages for Prosciutto di Parma on one menu, including a 30-month-old Parma Ham. Other specialities include a soufflé of Parmigiano Reggiano and a tagliatelle with Cutello di Zibello.

Ristorante La Forchetta, Borgo S. Biagio, 6, 43121 Parma (PR). Open for lunch and dinner seven days a week. Closed Tuesday.

(http://www.laforchettaparma.it/la-forchetta.php#)

Ristorante Gallo D'Oro

Part of the restaurant group Tipico a Tavola (http://www.tipicoatavola.com/). Not quite a chain, but a group of restaurants that banned together in Emilia Romagna to focus on preserving the traditional cuisine of the region. Gallo D'Oro, or golden rooster, offers a large closed-in patio overlooking the pedestrian-friendly street. Large platters of Prosciutto di Parma, served with warm and fluffy torta fritta, precede a trio of tortelli—offering the option to taste different versions including pumpkin, butter, and sage. A plate of only six tortelli seems small when it arrives, but fills the belly quickly.

Ristorante Gallo D'Oro, Borgo della Salina, 3, 43121 Parma (PR.) Look for the rooster outside. Closed Sunday for dinner.

(http://www.gallodororistorante.it/)

Antica Osteria della Ghiaia

A little more kitsch than the other Parma recommendations, but still reliable, even after over 60 years of continuous operation. They offer a simple two course menu with a pasta and a plate of mixed salumi and torta fritta for only €15. They pride themselves on their cappelletti in brodo, or be adventurous and order the horse tartare.

Antica Osteria della Ghiaia, Borgo Paggeria 12, 43121, Parma, (PR). Open six days a week for lunch and dinner. Closed Monday.

(http://www.osteriadellaghiaia.it/)

Sorelle Picchi Trattoria Salumeria

Sorelle Picchi offers a prime location on the main shopping street of Parma, and although a little more expensive than options just a few blocks away, it's a perfect spot for people watching in Parma. Heavy on the truffles, antipasti include a red potato pie layered with cheese and truffles. Pastas include a fettuccine or risotto with truffles. Also on offer is a tasting of Parmigiano Reggiano, including cheese from three different kinds of cows, including mountain cows, plains cows, and the rare red cow.

Sorelle Picchi Trattoria Salumeria, Strada Luigi Carlo Farini, 27, 43100 Parma (PR). Open seven days a week for lunch and dinner.

(http://www.trattoriasorellepicchi.com/sorellepicchi/)

Outside of Parma

Antica Corte Palla Vicina Relais

Representing the Parma lowlands cuisine, one Michelin Star Antica Corte Palla Vicina lies on the banks of the Po River, almost into Lombardy. Famous for its historic wine and salumi cellars, and award-wining culatello. Chef Massimo Spigaroli offers an impressive tasting menu, which changes with the seasons. This is a restaurant worth driving to.

Antica Corte Palla Vicina Relais, Strada del Palazzo Due Torri, 3, 43010, Polesine Parmense (PR). €€€ Tasting menus start at €86 Euros, or €115 with Emilia Romagna wine pairings. Closed Monday and for the month of January.

(http://www.anticacortepallavicinarelais.com/)

If this seems pricey, try Al Cavallino Bianco, a more affordable bistro run by Chef Spigaroli's brother, Luciano

(http://www.ristorantealcavallinobianco.it/).

Ristorante Colombo

Also located in Polesine Parmense, but a more affordable option. Ristorante Colombo is a family-run trattoria focusing on Emilian Cuisine. It is also a Michelin Guide recommended restaurant.

Ristorante Colombo Via Magadiscio,103, Polesine Parmense (PR). No website or Facebook page, but can be contacted for hours and reservations (+39052498114).

Hostaria da Ivan

With a dining room overlooking a small garden, the menu specializes in local, seasonal cuisine, including roasted meats and potatoes. They also offer some more innovative versions of local dishes. Hostaria da Ivan is known in Parma for offering the world's first Salumi Therapy (http://www.salumoterapia.it/), which focuses on the ritual of the salumi.

Hostaria da Ivan, Via Villa 24, Fontanella di Roccabianca (PR). Open for lunch and dinner five days a week. They are closed Monday and Tuesday.

(http://www.hostariadaivan.it/)

In and Around Piacenza

Ristorante la Carrozza

Popular restaurant within the city of Piacenza, known for a friendly environment and unique dishes, including a risotto served in a wheel of cheese.

Ristorante la Carrozza, Via X Giugno, 122, 29121 Piacenza (PC). Open for lunch and dinner seven days a week. The restaurant has no website and no Facebook page, and can be difficult to find. Walk towards the northeast edge of town, almost to the river. If you walk into Lombardy, you've gone too far.

Agriturismo La Favorita

Located about a half hour south of Piacenza, this agriturismo offers rooms, typical local cuisine, and horseback riding. They specialize in fresh baked breads as well as their own beef, which comes from their land.

Agriturismo La Favorita, Localita' Bicchignano, 29020 Villò di Vigolzone (PC). Open for dinner Wednesday through Sunday, closed Monday and Tuesday.

(http://www.agriturismolafavorita.it/)

Trattoria Cattivelli

Located in the little town of Monticelli d'Ongina, about 30 minutes east of Piacenza, and surrounded by the Po River. The town is home to the annual garlic festival. The restaurant has an outdoor setting overlooking the river and the countryside. The menu is uber-local, including seafood specialities from the Po, such as marinated eel and freshwater sturgeon, along with Piacenza specialties like Culatello di Zibello.

Trattoria Cattivelli, Via Chiesa di Isola Serafini, 2, 29010 Monticelli d'Ongina (PC). Open five days a week for dinner, they are closed on Tuesday and Wednesday.

(http://www.trattoriacattivelli.it)

Ristorante Il Castellaccio

A Michelin Guide recommended restaurant located about 25 minutes south of Piacenza, along the Trebbia River. The restaurant is set inside a castle dating to 1400 and is a little more refined than others recommended in the area. An entire section of the menu focuses on white truffles, but in this case they are from nearby Alba instead of Emilia Romagna. Dishes focus on a mix of tradition and contemporary, of Piacenza and nearby Lombardy.

Ristorante Il Castellaccio, Marchesi di Travo, Rivergaro (PC). Even being a little more sophisticated, pastas are generally less than €15 making Il Castellaccio a good value. Closed Tuesday and Wednesday.

(http://www.castellaccio.it/)

In and Around Romagna

Rimini

Osteria La Sangiovesa

Traditional restaurant well known for its versions of Romagna cuisine, including passatelli served with cured meats and dried tomatoes, and rabbit cacciatore. They also have a shop where you can purchase local specialities.

Osteria La Sangiovesa, Piazza Beato Simone Balacchi, 14, 47822 Santarcangelo di Romagna (RN). Open for dinner six days a week, and open for lunch and dinner on Sunday.

(http://www.sangiovesa.it/en/)

Ristorante Vite

A unique concept in Emilia Romagna, Vite offers second chances to local youth who have been affected by drugs. They train people in hospitality and culinary arts in their restaurant, and prepare them to enter the workforce. They have very good food too, with a slightly more contemporary offering. Vite also offers different tasting menus, including a vegetarian tasting, all with wine pairings.

Ristorante Vite, Via Monte Pirolo, 7, 47853 Coriano (RN). Open six days a week for lunch and dinner. Closed on Tuesday.

(http://www.ristorantevite.it/en)

Ristorante Zaghini

Serving Romagnola cuisine since 1895, and known locally as the temple of tagliatelle al ragù. Also serves piadina, and is known historically for its perfectly cooked grilled chicken.

Ristorante Zaghini, Piazza A. Gramsci, 14, 47822 Santarcangelo de Romagna (RN). Open for lunch and dinner six days a week. Closed on Monday.

(http://www.ristorantezaghini.it/)

Forli-Cesena

Eataly Forli

The Forli branch of Eataly hosts Trattoria di Giuliana on one of the upper floors, with views over the town piazza. Giuliana, and her husband, Moreno, are there to host most days, along with their daughter, who currently runs the restaurant. Previously, Giuliana and Moreno ran Locanda al Gambero Rosso, which for 60 years specialized in *cucina povera*, the Italian food of the poor, and of the countryside. Currently, they consult on the restaurant at Eataly to ensure the dishes are true to the local traditions and protect culinary heritage. Must eats include their famous meatballs, and a starter of liver pâté, two dishes many people would overlook. If Moreno is in, and the season is right, ask about the green herb soup that they offer. Moreno forages for the local herbs himself and it is a true treat.

Eataly Forli, Piazza Saffi Aurelio, 45, 47121 Forlì (FC). Open for lunch and dinner seven days a week.

(http://www.eataly.net/it_it/negozi/forli/)

Corte San Ruffillo

The restaurant at Corte San Ruffillo is located just outside the small village of Dovadola, south of Forli, on the road to Florence. It is another restaurant that falls squarely into the category "well worth the drive." It is hard to make recommendations for particular dishes at Corte San Ruffillo, as they change their menu so frequently. The menu is a perfect mix of tradition and contemporary influences, all set inside the original stone walls of an old farm house, decorated with a modern flair. In the early spring it might be cappelletti with wild herb sauce and fresh peas, or in the fall a tagliatelle with wild board ragù. Venison carpaccio, roast duck, or slow roasted lamb shoulder, all made with local ingredients, might also be offered.

Corte San Ruffillo, Via San Ruffillo 1, 47013 Dovadola (FC). Open for dinner Wednesday through Saturday, with the possibility of a lunch by reservation only. Open for lunch and dinner on Sunday. Closed Monday and Tuesday. Drive south from Dovadola a few kilometers, and follow the sign on the left for Corte San Ruffillo.

(http://www.cortesanruffillo.it/en/)

Trattoria Montepaolo

Traditional Romagna cuisine, often with modern interpretations. Chef Francisco studied in France, offering a unique use of local ingredients. In the spring, the focus is on artichokes. In the fall, it's on mushrooms. In November, they celebrate the truffle. The ambience borders on kitsch, but the service is friendly and the view is inspirational.

Trattoria Montepaolo, Via Monte Paolo, 55, 47013 Dovadola (FC). Google Maps is way wrong on this one. When you think you've gone too far, keep going. It is a good couple kilometers from the main road, at the very top of the hill, with a lovely view over the valley during the day. Closed Monday. During summer months, open for dinner Tuesday through Sunday, and lunch on Saturday and Sunday with a reservation. During the winter they are open on Tuesday, by reservation only.

(http://www.trattoriamontepaolo.it/)

Ristorante La Buca

Chef Stefano Bartolini's Michelin Star seafood restaurant along the canals of Cesenatico, where he personally chooses the fish for the menu each and every day. The singular focus of the menu is on fresh fish and seafood, in a contemporary presentation, without forgoing tradition. In fact, it is hard to find a dish on the menu that is not fish-centric. The menu is complimented by an extensive international wine list.

La Buca, €€€, Corso Garibaldi, 48, 47042 Cesenatico (FC) Open six days a week for lunch and dinner. Closed Monday. Reservations recommended at least three days in advance. Tasting menus start at €68 per person.

(http://www.labucaristorante.com/?lang=en)

Trattoria dell'Autista

Rustic dining at its best. It doesn't get more traditional Romagnola than Trattoria dell'Autista in Savignano Sul Rubicone with fresh pasta, grilled meats, and local truffles.

Trattoria dell'Autista, Via Cesare Battisti, 20, 47039 Savignano Sul Rubicone (FC). Open six days a week from 12:00 – 9:00 pm. Closed on Sunday.

Ravenna

L'Acciuga

Translating to "the anchovy," L'Acciuga focuses on local seafood, and, of course, anchovies. Chef Matthew offers a contemporary take on local cuisine, offering crudité and raw fish dishes, along with local pasta specialities like cappelletti and cod. They even rolled out a food truck of sorts that can be rented out for parties and corporate events.

L'Acciuga, Viale Francesco Baracca 74, 48121 Ravenna (RA). Open every day for lunch and dinner.

(http://www.osterialacciuga.it/)

Antica Trattoria Al Gallo 1909

Behind a Byzantine facade, with Art Deco stained glass and an Art Nouveau-inspired decor bordering on kitsch, "The Gallo" offers homemade pasta, Adriatic fish, and local produce. Destroyed during World War II, the restaurant was rebuilt, now run by the third generation of the Turicchia family.

Antica Trattoria Al Gallo 1909, €€€, Via Maggiore 87, 48123 Ravenna (RA). Open for lunch and dinner Wednesday, Thursday, Friday, and Saturday, and lunch only on Sunday. Closed Monday and Tuesday.

(http://www.algallo1909.it/)

Ca 'de Ven

If there is one touristy restaurant in Ravenna, this is it. On everyone's must-visit list in Ravenna because of its history. There are rumors that Dante stepped foot inside the palace before it became a restaurant. Just be on guard. Servers have a tendency to engage in a little price gauging with tourists, particularly with respect to bottles of wine. Ask to see the wine list before ordering a bottle. The list is not offered automatically.

Ca 'de Ven, Via Corrado Ricci 24, 48100 Ravenna (RA). Tasting menus, including wine, start at €38 per person. Due to its popularity, reservations are recommended. Open for lunch and dinner. Closed Monday.

(http://www.cadeven.it/)

Brisighella

Ristorante La Rocca

Recently renovated in a contemporary style, but La Rocca plays to its traditional setting, under the arches of Via delle Volte in Brisighella. The location of the village, in the shadows of Tuscany, means the menu is focused on Tuscan-Romagna cuisine, and local DOP olive oil.

Ristorante La Rocca, Via delle Volte 10, Brisighella (RA). Open for lunch and dinner seven days a week. La Rocca also offers a business lunch during the week.

(http://www.albergo-larocca.it/ristorante)

Ristorante la Grotta

Set inside an actual grotto, or cave, Ristorante la Grotta earns points for its location, with arched ceilings and ancient, exposed stone walls. During the day they offer a great value lunch menu, which arrives on a handwritten piece of paper, in Italian. Four course set meals start at €29 for dinner.

Ristorante la Grotta, Via Antonio Metelli, 1, 48013 Brisighella (RA). Open for lunch and dinner six days a week. Closed Wednesday, although open for dinner on Wednesday during the summer.

(http://www.ristorante-lagrotta.it/)

Ferrara

Trattoria Il Mandolino

Traditional Ferrarese cuisine in a typical environment in the center of the Medieval quarter. Eclectic artwork covers almost every inch of the walls. The menu focuses on handmade egg pasta, local wines including Trebbiano and Sangiovese, and very local cured meats.

Trattoria Il Mandolino, Via Carlo Mayr, 83, 44121 Ferrara (FE). Open for lunch and dinner Wednesday through Sunday and for lunch only on Monday. Closed Tuesday. And, the true sign of an un-touristy restaurant, Il Mandolino closes during the summer holiday, from the end of June until the middle of August.

(http://www.ristoranteilmandolino.it/)

Al Brindisi

Translating to "the toast," it claims to be one of the oldest wine bars in the world. Dating to 1435, Al Brindisi is found in a narrow alley near the Cathedral. The *Menu del Lavoro*, or working menu, starts at only €15 for a salad, pasta, and glass of wine. The most elaborate tasting menu runs €50 a person, but can hardly be considered a working man's menu. It's a must-visit in Ferrara.

Al Brindisi, Via Guglielmo degli Adelardi, 11, 44121 Ferrara (FE). Open all day, six days a week. Closed Monday.

(http://www.albrindisi.net/)

Mordicchio La Piadina

Perfect spot for cheap Romagna eats, including, obviously, piadina with cured meats and cheeses.

Mordicchio La Piadina, Piazza Sacrati 3, Ferrara (FE). Open for lunch Monday through Saturday, and dinner on Monday, Tuesday, Wednesday, Friday, and Saturday. Closed on Sunday.

14

GENERAL TRAVEL RESOURCES

Now that Emilia Romagna calls your name, it's important to know how to travel in Emilia Romagna. This chapter includes the details on how to travel to Emilia Romagna, how to travel around the region, when to visit, and recommendations on tour experiences.

Flying To Emilia Romagna

The easiest way to get to Emilia Romagna from an international destination is to fly, either to Bologna or Milan. Although there are a handful of smaller airports, including those in Parma and Rimini, there are very few international connections. Most flights are within Europe, and even then only operate seasonal flights on discount carriers like Ryan Air.

Milan Malpensa Airport offers more international arrivals than Bologna airport, but poses some challenges when it comes to transport into Emilia Romagna. Travelers who rent a car at Milan airport can be in Bologna in about two hours and to Parma in only one hour.

Travelers who do not rent a car to explore Emilia Romagna can get to their destination by train, although it's a little more complicated. The best way is to take either a bus or a train from Milan Airport to the main train station, Milano Centrale. The Malpensa Express (http://www.malpensaexpress.it/en/) train runs every 30 minutes. It's best to check the time table ahead of time. There are several bus companies that run services from the airport to Milano Centrale as well. They are about the same price as the train, but the train is more convenient for transferring to connecting trains. Once at Milano Centrale, either via bus or train, you can travel by train from Milan to Bologna, or other destinations.

It can take about three to four hours to travel by train from the Milan airport to the cities along the Via Emilia, sometimes longer. Although it takes less time to train from the Milan train station, adding in the time from the airport just adds to the total trip time. Be prepared on the return to ensure you have sufficient time to catch departing flights from Milan Malpensa. You might consider spending the night in Milan (or better, near the airport), to catch early departures. Check out Marriott's Moxy Hotel at the Milan airport for a trendy and comfortable airport stay.

Although Milan airport has more international connections, flying into Marconi Airport in Bologna is much easier. Located only six kilometers from the city center, it's a quick taxi or bus ride into town, or to the train station. Bologna airport connects to many cities around Europe, making it a one-stop destination from the U.S. with connections through Amsterdam, Frankfurt, London, and Paris. Emirates recently launched direct flights from Bologna to Dubai, which then connects Emilia Romagna to the rest of Asia and Africa.

How to Get Around Emilia Romagna

There are two main ways to explore Emilia Romagna: by rental car or train. There are bus connections throughout the area, but buses can be more complicated.

Driving in Italy can be a challenge, but it *is* the best way to explore the nooks and crannies of Emilia Romagna. It enables a traveler to stay in an agriturismo, to explore the food producers and wineries outside of the main towns, and offers the opportunity to eat at some amazing restaurants that are only accessible by car.

There are a few things to take into consideration when deciding whether to rent a car to drive around Emilia Romagna. First, rent a car with GPS or ensure you have a great smart phone with a local sim card or international data plan. It's nearly impossible, or at the least minimally frustrating, to follow road maps when exploring the countryside.

Second, if you plan to stay predominantly in the larger cities, parking can be a problem. Hotels might offer parking at an extra fee, or they can recommend where to park, as many city centers are pedestrian only. Most rental cars will include a blue parking disc on the windshield. This is used to track how long you park in restricted areas. For example, if a parking spot is limited to two hours, the disc is set for the time the car is parked; that way, the local police can control parking.

Train service is extensive in Italy, and can be a convenient way to explore all of the main cities and towns. Relying solely on train travel, though, makes it more challenging to explore the countryside. If you plan ahead of time, it's possible to buy train tickets online, which will often be cheaper than buying tickets at the station day of. (This is particularly the case for longer journeys.) When purchasing tickets online, you will be given an electronic ticket that will be scanned by the conductor on the train. The conductor might ask for identification as well, but this is rare.

Allow extra time to find your train platform, as stations can be a little confusing. The numbering of train platforms is not always intuitive and it is not always possible to find an English speaker for help. Welcome to travel in Italy! This is particularly the case in Bologna, one of the largest train stations in Italy. Platforms are marked with a number, or a number and letter. For example, Platform 3 is different from Platform 3W, which is a tiny platform, set off to one side of the station, and again, hard to find.

Also, don't forget to validate your ticket at a machine on the platform, or at the base of the stairs before heading up to the platform. A ticket without validation might lead to a fine.

Even if a traveler decides not to rent a car, there are a few ways to explore the countryside, by using tour companies and culinary tour operators.

When to Go to Emilia Romagna

The winter months in much of Emilia Romagna can be harsh, with the possibility of snow and definitely a wind and chill to the air. On the opposite end of the spectrum, summer can be hot, and air conditioning is not as plentiful as it is in the United States. August travel should be avoided, as much of the country goes on holiday. Many cities virtually shut down during Ferragosto, in the days surrounding August 15.

The best time to visit Emilia Romagna is in the spring or fall. Spring weather is lovely, and the countryside is just starting to wake. The fall brings the harvest, and is a great opportunity to perhaps witness a wine harvest. It is also the best time to experience fall truffles and mushrooms. There also are more food and wine related festivals during May, June, September, October, and November.

Something to remember when traveling anywhere in Italy: Sundays. Things are quiet on Sundays. Many restaurants are closed and services are limited. No matter where you are, plan ahead. This might be a good day to stay at an agriturismo. Ensure they have an open restaurant and enjoy a big Sunday meal in the countryside. Alternatively, choose to stay in one of the larger, more touristed areas to ensure restaurants are open. Great places for Sunday stays include Bologna, Modena, and Parma.

Discover Ferrari & Pavarotti Land

One of the challenges of traveling in Emilia Romagna is that most of the best food and wine producers, and therefore food experiences, are outside of the main towns. Yes, it is easy to travel by train from one town to another. But, many of the producers are out in the countryside.

As part of the 2015 EXPO in Milan, the Modena tourism board realized this was a problem and decided to try out something new. They offered something akin to a hop-on, hop-off bus to explore the land of fast cars and slow food. Technically, the passport was called Discover Ferrari & Pavarotti Land: Modena, Slow Food, Fast Cars. But, it's more commonly known as Discover Ferrari. Much easier to swallow.

Discover Ferrari is a route of Modena food and wine producers, along with some historic sites, which surround the town of Modena. There is a route map, which you can explore using your own transportation, or by using the hop-on, hop off bus system. Each of the stops offers a free tour or tasting, allowing tourists the chance to try the major Modena foods. This includes Parmigiano Reggiano, Lambrusco, Prosciutto di Modena, and balsamic vinegar. The tour also includes the Ferrari Museums in Maranello and Modena, and Pavarotti's house and museum.

What makes this tour even better is that all of these stops promise to be open seven days a week, even in August. That means it is unnecessary to call ahead to make arrangements for visits. Traveling Italy in August can be a pain; this makes exploring the region during the summer a lot more predictable.

Although originally created to coincide with 2015 EXPO Milan, the tourism board continued the offering during 2016. As of publication, the route is still available for 2017. The passport can be purchased ahead of time on the Discover Ferrari website or at the Museo Enzo Ferrari in Modena. You can start the tour in Modena, or even at the Bologna and Reggio Emilia high speed train stations, which means it's possible to explore the best of Modena, even when based in Bologna.

The passport costs €48, and is valid for 48 consecutive hours. It includes the cost of entry to the museums and businesses along the route. A children's passport is also available for €24. Children under 5 are free. Although available every day, "every day" does not include Christmas Eve, Christmas Day, or New Years Day.

(http://www.ferraripavarottiland.it/eu-en/default.aspx)

FICO Eataly World

Scheduled to open in the fall of 2017, Eataly World promises to be the world's first food amusement park. From the creators of Eataly, the "FICO" in the title stands for Fabbrica Italiana Contadina, or Italian farming factory. The focus is really on eating and, more importantly, on food production.

Located just outside of the Bologna city center, Eataly World will include 80,000 square meters of food culture and education about Italian cuisine. Approximately 10% of the square footage will be reserved for restaurants; amazingly, twice that amount will be focused on food cultivation and farming. It will be possible to see specific breeds of cows, learn what they eat, how they are milked, and how their milk becomes Parmigiano Reggiano. You'll be able to taste the cheese at one of the restaurants, and bring some home from one of the shops. Expect workshops, training programs, and cooking classes as well. Eataly World is set to revolutionize culinary tourism in Emilia Romagna.

Eataly World, Via Paolo Canali, 1, 40127 Bologna (BO). Eataly World has been "in the works" for quite some time. Although they expect a September 2017 opening, check their website for up-to-date information before traveling to Bologna. (http://eatalyworld.it/en/home)

Culinary Experiences in Emilia Romagna

Helena from Yummy Italy, is as an expert on DOP and IGP products, and all things food in Emilia Romagna. Yummy Italy offers customized culinary experiences, one of the best in the area, with a focus on sustainable producers whenever possible. She prides herself on her knowledge of the different specialty foods that are certified in the region, and is a certified sommelier, certified balsamic vinegar taster, and certified cheese taster. Helena offers specialized and customized programs that include cookery courses, gourmet experiences, wine trails, and more to help travelers explore the region in depth. Yummy Italy also offers culinary experiences for food professionals—aimed at chefs, winemakers, and restaurateurs to give them an even more in-depth experience. (http://www.yummy-italy.com/)

Bologna Welcome, the tourism office of Bologna, provides information regarding food-related tours and classes. Experiences include wine tours of the area, cooking classes, and walking tours within the city. Some of the programs are offered daily, but others are offered at set times. Some tours start for as little as €25, and you can book directly from their website. (http://www.bolognawelcome.com/en/)

Modenatur is a tour operator that works closely with the Emilia Romagna Tourism Board. They can help book various kinds of tours, including tickets for Discover Ferrari. They also offer a list of recommended quality restaurants in and around Modena. They can arrange visits to various producers, including Parmigiano Reggiano, Lambrusco, Aceto Balsamico, and Prosciutto di Modena, and can arrange hands-on cooking classes or cooking demonstrations, from half day programs to multiple day courses. Modenatur can organize food and wine tours by bus, or car hire. (http://www.modenatur.it/)

The Parma tourism office offers similar recommendations for half-day tours, which take food tourists outside of the city to food producers in the surrounding area. Most tours include a visit to a Prosciutto di Parma producer, and are conducted by either bus or bike. (http://www.turismo.comune.parma.it/en/)

Culinary Events in Emilia Romagna

With the number of DOP and IGP products sprinkled throughout the region, it is no surprise that Emilia Romagna is host to food and wine related events and festivals throughout the year. Although earlier in the year, events are less common due to weather, plenty of events are on offer during the spring, summer, and fall months.

The best resource for the schedule of events is Emilia Romagna's Food Valley official website

(http://www.winefoodemiliaromagna.com/events).

Eventie Sagre is another website that collects information on all of the festivals throughout Italy. This website is not dedicated merely to food and wine festivals the way the Food Valley's website is, but you can sort by region, month, and type of festival.

(http://www.eventiesagre.it/home.html).

Information on many of these festivals can be spotty online. The best bet is to ask at the local tourism office, or at your hotel, about specific details.

Spring Festivals – May, June, and July

Wild Asparagus: During the first week in May, in Vezzano sul Crostolo, in Reggio Emilia, this festival honors wild asparagus. Asparagus is offered in many different food specialties including ravioli and fried dumplings.

(http://www.comune.vezzano-sul-crostolo.re.it/)

Cherries: Held at the end of May, in San Leo in Rimini, the annual Cherry Festival boasts food stands and music performances to celebrate the local cherries. Events are held along the river banks.

(http://www.lavalmarecchia.it)

Outdoor Dining: Generally held in June, "Brisighella Romantica" is a special occasion for outdoor candlelight dinners, in the heart of the town. To make this event even more unique, in addition to a special menu, there are also exhibitions and musical entertainment with the theme of love. It is more than just tables set outside of restaurants. Instead, tables are set up in the middle of the streets!

(http://www.brisighella.org/en/)

Mushrooms and Pasta: In June, Rimini hosts two different food-related festivals. Miratoio di Pennabilli hosts a festival in honor of the *prugnolo*, the St. George's mushroom. (http://www.sagradelprugnolo.org/) Poggio Berni hosts a Tagliatelle festival, with opportunities to try fresh tagliatelle with the St. George's mushroom.

(http://www.lavalmarecchia.it)

Bread: Held in late June, Maiolo hosts La Festa del Pane, a two-day festival focused on the traditional breads of Rimini and the surrounding area. Maiolo also houses a Bread Museum, and the Bread Festival highlights the history of cooking breads at home, in farmhouse ovens, using local flours, and traditional methods. Unique to other festivals, there are opportunities for visitors to spend evenings in the farmyards of country houses where meals are prepared with local bread, flowers, and herbs.

(http://www.adriacoast.com/ita-eventi-1.php)

Lambrusco: During June, Albinea in Reggio Emilia hosts the Festival of Lambrusco. It is a four-day affair celebrating the history and tradition of Lambrusco.

(http://www.sagralambrusco.it/)

Artusi and Italian Food: One of the biggest and most important festivals in Emilia Romagna is held during the last week of June and first week of July. It is the Festa Artusiana held in Forlimpopoli. For many of the other, smaller festivals, you can just show up and explore the small village hosting the event. For the Festa Artusiana, it is important to plan ahead, particularly to secure accommodations in Forlimpopoli.

(http://www.festartusiana.it/)

Good Food: During the end of July, Torriana near Rimini hosts the Scorticata, or the Hillside of Pleasure. It is a celebration of flavors and good foods. Not only does the festival highlight local foods, there is an international element, as well. Expect beer and wine tastings, along with cheeses, cold cuts, cakes, chocolate, and olive oils.

(https://www.facebook.com/scorticata/)

Fall Festivals – September, October, and November

Honey: During the first week of September, the ancient village of Montebello in Rimini hosts their annual Honey Festival. The festival honors local honey production, and includes a live demonstration of honey extraction.

(http://en.riviera.rimini.it/situr/events)

Parma Ham: The Prosciutto di Parma Consortium hosts a Prosciutto festival at the beginning of September each year. Many of the production facilities open their doors to visitors. There is even a slicing contest.

(http://www.festivaldelprosciuttodiparma.com/en/)

Coppa: During September, Piacenza hosts the Coppa Festival outside of the city. The festival marks the end of the summer season with food stalls, typical local products, music, and fireworks.

(http://www.festadellacoppa.it)

Salt: During early September, Cervia hosts the Taste of Salt. Salt saved the day centuries ago, when it was used as a preserving agent to lengthen the life of food. It was therefore called "white gold" in the Cervian economy. This festival highlights salt with exhibitions, shows, wine, food, and special dishes.

(http://www.cerviasaporedisale.it)

Polenta: On Sundays throughout September, Perticara in Rimini hosts the Festival of Polenta. The celebration is not limited to polenta, though, and also highlights wild mushrooms and berries. The polenta itself is generally served with sausage, wild boar, or wild porcini mushrooms.

(http://www.sagreinromagna.it/sagre/3636/)

Eels: During the end of September, Comacchio in Ferrara hosts an annual eel festival. The festival offers eel-based recipes, boat rides around the lagoon, and local restaurants offer eel specialties.

(http://www.sagradellanguilla.it)

Sangiovese: During the end of October, Giovinbacco in Piazza, in Ravenna, hosts The Big Food and Wine Festival in Romagna. You just have to love the name. This is the biggest event dedicated to Romagna Sangiovese, as well as other wines of Romagna. Visitors are able to taste "dozens and dozens" of wines at the festival held in town squares. Squares are dedicated to the foods of Romagna, including piadina, cheese, and even craft beer.

(www.giovinbacco.it/info/accoglienza)

Mortadella: During October, the Mortadella Bologna Consortium hosts the MortadellaBo Festival, which offers tastings and cooking classes, and even crowns a mortadella queen.

(http://www.mortadellabologna.com/)

Pork: During November, several towns throughout Parma hold their annual November Porc festival, known as "Let's Hope It's Foggy in Parma." The festival is dedicated to the "foggy pork" products of Parma. Competitions are held, including a regional pork competition referred to as the "greediest salami competition in Italy." Producers compete for different titles including the biggest, heaviest, longest, etc. all while promoting the flavors of Parma. Participating towns include Sissa, Polesine Parmense, Roccabianco, and Zibello. There is also rumor of some salami throwing.

(http://www.novemberporc.com)

Food and Wine: During November, Imola hosts Baccanale, a

16-day festival including exhibitions, markets, food, and wine, along with several food routes focused on the dishes and tradition of Imola.

(http://www.baccanaleimola.it/)

Cave Cheese: During the end of November, and into early December, Sogliano al Rubicone in Forli-Cesena celebrates cave cheese. The festival events are held to coincide with the time of year the pits are carefully opened to reveal the aged cheese held inside. During the festival, the town offers the opportunity to buy and taste other typical local products.

(http://www.comune.sogliano.fc.it/)

Cave Cheese: During the second and third Sunday in November, Ambra di Talamello in Rimini also hosts a cave cheese festival. The festival celebrates the cheese and the food products that are paired with it. This particular pit cheese is referred to as Ambra, or Amber, after the color it turns after the maturing phase. The fair offers cheese tasting and sales.

(http://www.comune.talamello.rn.it/)

Wine: Usually during the third week of November, Enologica, Emilia Romagna's biggest wine exhibit, takes place in Bologna. Organized by Enoteca Regionale, the festival represents all of the wines produced around the region.

(http://www.enologica.org/)

Wine: Held just after Enologica, over 250 winemakers from all over Italy participate in the Mercato Dei Vini Dei Vignaioli Indipendenti in Piacenza. The goal is to promote artisanal wines and offer boutique wineries an opportunity to showcase their products.

(http://www.mercatodeivini.it/)

Olive Oil: During the last weekend of November, Brisighella hosts the Olive Tree and Olive Oil Festival. Held in the epicenter of olive oil production in Emilia Romagna, the festival offers music, entertainment, and a market where olive oils are offered for taste and for sale.

(http://www.brisighella.org/en/)

Fall Truffle and Mushroom Festivals

From late September through October and into November, the entire region goes mushroom and truffle crazy. There are more festivals focused on these products than any one person can attend. The Emilia Romagna Tourism Board generally provides information on them all each year.

(http://www.emiliaromagnaturismo.com/en/)

During the middle of September, in San Giorgio Piacentino, expert mushroom gatherers from the area around Piacenza face off in the Mushroom Fair and Mushroom Gather Palio. Yes, a *"palio,"* or race, of mushroom gatherers. Traditional markets exhibit mushrooms, along with food stands and music.

(http://turismo.provincia.piacenza.it/index.php)

During the second half of September, in the Parma Apennines, is a fair dedicated to the Borgotaro mushroom, an IGP porcini mushroom. Held in the towns of Borgo Val di Tara, Albareto, and Pontremoli, it includes two weeks of cultural events, entertainment, and, of course, mushrooms.

(http://www.sagradelfungodiborgotaro.it/)

During October, Sant'Agata Feltria hosts the National White Truffle Fair. Sant'Agata Feltria is a small village in the province of Rimini, north-east of San Marino. In addition to truffles, the festival highlights other seasonal products, including mushrooms, honey, herbs, and chestnuts, as well as handmade products.

(http://www.santagatainfiera.com/en_homepage.asp)

Truffle, Bread, and Ferrarese Pearls Festival: More truffle fun in Bondeno, in Ferrara. Held in the middle of October, over two weeks, the festival is dedicated to the truffle, bread, and local products from the area. These products are the "pearls" on offer. It is an opportunity to experience a gastronomic festival that also highlights the local bread, Coppia Ferrarese.

(http://www.tartufopaneperle.it; http://www.fieradelpane.it)

During weekends throughout October and November, one of the largest fall festivals is TartuFesta in the Bologna Hills. Bologna hosts a series of white truffle-related events throughout the Bologna Hills. The heart of the truffle festival includes the events held in Savigno, the Citta del Tartufo, and Sasso Marconi, which also sees displays of Italian food products.

(http://www.provincia.bologna.it/tartufesta)

During the last two weeks of November, Sant'Agostino in Ferrara hosts the Autumn Truffle Festival honoring the prestigious white truffle. As part of the festival, it's possible to tour the local Panfilia Woods in search of truffles.

(http://www.ferraraterraeacqua.it/en/events)

December

Although December is a slow month for food festivals, towns and villages throughout Emilia Romagna host Christmas markets. If you can handle the cold, it's a lovely time to be in Italy.

Zampone: Although Italians are focused on preparing for Christmas during the month of December, they still find time to celebrate giant, stuffed pig trotters. Castelnuovo Rangone, near Modena, hosts Super Zampone, promoting the largest zampone in the world. The zampone is cooked in the main square in a large stainless steel pot. Generally zampone takes a long time to cook, so cooking a giant one takes even longer…about three days. Apparently, the zampone weighs more and more each year.

(http://zampone.com/)

Sample Itineraries

This book lays out a road map for independent exploration of Emilia Romagna. But, sometimes you need a little help in coming up with an itinerary. Here are some suggestions for 7 day itineraries:

The Holy Trinity of Emilia Romagna: The "starter" itinerary for Emilia Romagna includes two nights each in Bologna, Modena, and Parma. While in Bologna, plan a day trip to explore the Bologna Hills wineries. While in Modena, plan a day trip to producers of Parmigiano Reggiano and traditional balsamic vinegar, or book a ticket for the Discover Ferrari tour. While in Parma, plan a day trip to Langhirano to taste Prosciutto di Parma. This itinerary explores many of the key DOP products, and can be completed without a car, by booking excursions ahead of time.

Exploring Romagna: Exploring the lesser known side of Emilia Romagna includes two nights in each of Ferrara, Ravenna, and Forli-Cesena. While in Romagna, explore the wineries, eat loads of seafood, and find a cave cheese producer! Learn about olive oil production in Brisighella and take a pasta making class at Casa Artusi in Forlimpopoli.

Decompressing in the Countryside: To go off the beaten path, rent a car and explore the countryside by staying two nights in three different agroturismi. Explore Modena from Garuti Vini, the Bologna Hills from Corte d'Aibo, and Romagna from Corte San Ruffillo. At each agriturismo, plan at least one meal at the property. While on property arrange for balsamic vinegar tastings and winery tours as well. The owners of the agroturismi are the most tuned in to what is happening nearby.

Emilia Romagna in Luxury: Stay and eat in luxury with two nights at each of three luxury properties. Explore Romagna from Palazzo Viviani in Montegridolfo and dine on fresh seafood at La Buca in Cesenatico. Explore Modena from the contemporary Opera O2 in Castelvetro di Modena, and book well in advance for a table at Osteria Francescana in Modena. Explore Parma from Antica Corte Palla Vicina Relais in Polescine Parmenese and eat famous culatello (and more) at their restaurant.

APPENDIX

As a recovering attorney, I loathe footnotes. I think they ruin the flow of reading. So, in this book, I did not include them. Most of the book is written from our first-hand experiences of traveling and eating in Emilia Romagna. To supplement the facts, I relied predominantly on the websites of the various tourism boards across Emilia Romagna, the websites for individual DOP and IGP products, and the websites of hotels, restaurants, and food providers.

For more information on culinary travel in Emilia Romagna, please consult the following websites. Most, but not all, offer English versions.

Regional Tourism Boards

Emilia Romagna Tourism

(http://www.emiliaromagnaturismo.it/en)

Bologna Welcome

(http://www.bolognawelcome.com/en/)

IAT Bologna Hills

(http://www.iatcollibolognesi.it/iatcollibolognesi/en/)

Visit Modena

(http://www.visitmodena.it/english)

Tourism Reggio Emilia

(http://turismo.comune.re.it/en/homepage)

Tourist Office of Parma

(http://www.turismo.comune.parma.it/en)

Piacere Piacenza

(http://www.piacerepiacenza.it/)

Rimini Tourism

(http://www.riminiturismo.it/en)

Tourism Forli-Cesena

(http://www.turismo.fc.it/)

Ravenna Tourism

(http://www.turismo.ra.it/eng/)

Ferrara Tourism

(http://www.ferrarainfo.com/en/)

Wine and Dine Routes

Most of the local tourism boards have supported wine and dine routes focusing on particular regions or specialties. Each website offers recommendations on food producers, restaurants, and where to stay along the route. Some of the websites are more advanced than others, with some only published in Italian.

Via Emilia

(http://visitviaemilia.it/)

Forli and Cesena:

The Wine and Flavor Route of Forli and Cesena in Romagna

(http://www.stradavinisaporifc.it/en/)

Imola:

The Wine and Flavor Route of Imola's Hills

(www.stradaviniesapori.it)

Modena:

Piacere Modena

(http://www.piaceremodena.it/)

Reggio Emilia:

The Wine and Flavor Route of the Scandiano and Canossa Hills

(http://www.stradaviniesapori.re.it/en/)

The Wine and Flavor Route of the Reggio Emilia Courts

(http://www.stradavinicortireggiane.it/)

Parma:

The Ham and Wine Route of Parma

(http://www.stradadelprosciutto.it/)

The Culatello Road

(http://www.stradadelculatellodizibello.it/it/)

The Porcini Mushroom Road

(http://www.stradadelfungo.it/)

Piacenza:

A Journey Along the River Po, through the land, waterways, and foods of the Bassa Piacentina

(www.stradadelpo.it)

The Wines and Flavors Trails of the Piacenza Hills

(www.stradadeicollipiacentini.it)

DOP and IGP Consortia

There are over 40 DOP and IGP products in Emilia Romagna, and each has their own consortium. Some of the consortia offer great resources on their websites on the history, certification, and tasting of their products. The best of the websites are included in this list.

Cheese

Parmigiano Reggiano Consorzio

(http://www.parmigianoreggiano.com)

Consorzio Tutela Grana Padano

(http://www.granapadano.it/?l=en)

Meat

Prosciutto di Parma

(http://www.prosciuttodiparma.com/en_UK/consortium)

Prosciutto di Modena

(http://www.consorzioprosciuttomodena.it/)

Consorzio Mortadella Bologna IGP

(http://www.mortadellabologna.com/)

Consorzio Piacenza Alimentare (Consortium that regulates Coppa Piacentina, Pancetta Piacentina, and Salame Piacentino)

(http://www.consorziopiacenzalimentare.com/en/piacenza-food-valley)

Consorzio Parma Alimentare (Consortium that regulates Parma ham, Parma coppa, and Culatello di Zibello)

(http://www.parmalimentare.net/)

Balsamic Vinegar

Balsamico di Modena

(http://www.consorziobalsamico.it/?lang=en)

Balsamico di Reggio Emilia

(http://www.acetobalsamicotradizionale.it/home_en.php)

Wine Resources

Learning about wine in Emilia Romagna is a bit of a challenge because there are so many varieties in so many individual, small regions. The best place to start is the Enoteca Regionale (http://www.enotecaemiliaromagna.it/en), but there are local consortia that also provide valuable tools and resources.

Consortium of Lambrusco of Modena

(http://www.tutelalambrusco.it/en/)

Consortium of the Lambrusco Brand

(http://www.lambrusco.net/en)

Consortium of the Wine of Romagna

(http://www.consorziovinidiromagna.it/en/about-us/)

Other Resources

Emilia Romagna Tourism's Blog

(http://blog.travelemiliaromagna.com/)

Discover Italy's Resources on Emilia Romagna

(http://www.italia.it/en/discover-italy/emilia-romagna.html)

CULINARY GLOSSARY

In today's day and age, every smart phone can be an Italian-English dictionary and Google Translate is a worthwhile download. But, to save time, or to help translate restaurant menus when no WiFi is available, below is a list of the most common Italian words you will see on a menu.

A

aceto balsamico: balsamic vinegar; look for Aceto Balsamico di Modena Tradizionale or Extravecchio

aceto di vino: wine vinegar, more common than aceto balsamico

affogato: a mixture of espresso and gelato, literally gelato drowned in coffee

aglio: garlic

agnello: lamb

anatra: duck

anolini: similar to a ravioli, stuffed with cheese or meats

antipasti: a starter or appetizer

arancia: orange

B

biscottino: biscuits, normally seen on a gelato or dessert menu

bollito misto: mixed plate of boiled meat

burro: butter

burtleina: a meat bread with the consistency of an omelet

C

cacao: cocoa

caffè: espresso

cappone: usually referring to the broth that is served with tortellini or cappelletti, which is made from a castrated rooster

cappelletti: smaller version of tortelloni, generally stuffed with ricotta cheese; during the holidays it is served in a meat broth

caramello al sale: salted caramel

carciofo: artichoke

carne di cervo: venison

carpaccio: sliced raw meat, normally beef

chisolini: deep fried bread fritter

ciliegia: cherry

cinghiale: wild boar

cioccolato: chocolate

cipolla: onion

cippolini: a type of onion, but smaller

colombaccio: wood pigeon

coniglio: rabbit

contorni: side dish, often a vegetable or potato

coppa: pork neck salami, with two versions: Coppa Piacentina DOP and Coppa di Parma IGP. Not to be confused with coppa di testa, which is head cheese

coppia ferrarese: twisted sour dough bread

cotechino: fresh ground pork sausage made with less tender cuts of meat

crema: cream, often referring to a sauce for pasta, or a typical gelato flavor

culatello: pear shaped cured meat, served sliced, the best being Culatello di Zibello

D

dolce: dessert

E

enoteca: wine shop and wine bar, often serving food

F

fegato: liver

fiordilatte: fresh milk, generally referring to a gelato flavor

formaggio: cheese

formaggio di fossa: cave or pit cheese

fragola: strawberry

funghi: mushrooms

G

garganelli: thinly rolled pasta, cut into squares, then rolled around a small wooden stick

gnocchi: pasta made with potato

gnocco fritto: fried, puffed bread, usually served in Modena

gramigna: hollow, curly, tube-like pasta, made by running the pasta through a machine that looks like a small sausage maker

granita: like an Italian ice; often made with fresh fruits

gras pista: pounded lard used as a meat topping for warmed bread

guanciale: cured pork cheek

L

latte: milk

limone: lemon

M

maiale: pork

manzo: beef

marubini: similar to a ravioli, stuffed with sausage and cheese

melanzana: eggplant

minestra: soup

mortadella: pale pink pork sausage served sliced, or in cubes

N

nocino: liquor made from hazelnuts

nocciola: hazelnuts

O

olio d'oliva: olive oil

osteria: less formal than a restaurant or trattoria

P

pancetta: more fatty than other cured porks: characterized by alternating ribbons of deep red and white

pancotto: poor man's lasagna, made with day old bread

pane: bread

pasticceria: pastry shop

passatelli: dense, rolled pasta, made with Parmigiano Reggiano

pesce: fish

pesto: meaning pressed or blended, in Emilia Romagna it is often fresh pancetta or lard blended with rosemary or garlic

piadina: thin, flat bread from Romagna

pollo: chicken

pomodoro: tomato

porchetta: stuffed pork

primi piatti: a pasta or risotto course, the first main course, or the "carb" course

R

ragù: meat sauce

ricotta: soft, fresh, mild cheese

S

saba: thick and sweet concentration of grape juice, often served on soft cheese

salame: a singular round of cured meat, often referring to Salame Cremona, Salami Piacentino, or Salamini Italiani

salami: the plural of salame

salsiccia: sausage

salumi: general word for cured meats

salumeria: Italian deli where cured meats are sold

salvia: sage

secondi: a meat or fish course; the second main course

spinaci: spinach

squacquerone: soft, fresh, spreadable cheese

stinco: roasted pork shin

stracciatella: milk-flavored gelato, marked with chocolate flakes

T

tagliatelle: a flat ribbon-like pasta, similar in shape to fettuccine

tartufo: truffle

tavola calda: cafeteria-style restaurant

tigelle: aka crescentine, a dense round meat bread

torta fritta: fried, puffed bread; normally from Parma

tortelloni: small half-moon shaped pasta, generally stuffed with cheese or meat, served in a cream sauce, drizzled with balsamic vinegar (Tortelloni Vecchia Modena), or a butter sage sauce

tortelli: similar to a ravioli. In Piacenza, it is often stuffed with ricotta and spinach (tortelli con la coda), which is longer and more twisted

tortellini: smaller version of tortelloni, traditionally served in a meat broth (tortellini in brodo) but also often offered in a cream sauce (crema)

trattoria: more formal than an osteria, but less formal than a restaurant

U

uovo: egg

V

visciole: sour cherry

vitello: veal

Z

zampone: stuffed pig's trotter

zucca: pumpkin

ABOUT THE AUTHOR

Having visited more than 70 countries (and still counting), Amber travels With Husband In Tow. Together, she and her husband, Eric, seek new adventures in food as they travel on their stomachs. Amber launched their culinary travel blog in 2012.

Amber is a recovering tax attorney from the largest law firm in the world. After practicing for ten years it was clear a change was needed. Her travel blog started as a way to keep friends and family informed of where in the world Amber and Eric were traveling. Then, it turned into a passion, a passion for eating, and helping others explore the world through food. "Food travel" became a way of life for them, and the culinary travel blog became an extension of this passion.

The couple splits their time between Asia and Europe. Amber loves the food in Asia – the combination of fresh ingredients, thoughtful preparation, and the fantastic mix of sweet, salty, sour, and spicy.

But, when in Asia, she misses Europe. The food. The wine. The history. Over the past four years Amber and Eric have clocked many hours dedicated to researching the food culture of Portugal, Spain, Ireland, and of course, Italy. But, Emilia Romagna really tugged at their heart strings. There was something about the undiscovered food region that made Emilia Romagna the obvious choice for her first culinary travel guide.

To follow Amber and Eric on their culinary travels, check out the With Husband In Tow blog, or follow them on social media:

With Husband In Tow:

www.withhusbandintow.com/

Facebook:

www.facebook.com/WithHusbandInTowFoodTravelBlog/

Instagram:

www.instagram.com/withhusbandintow/

Twitter:

twitter.com/HusbandInTow

Or, sign up for the With Husband In Tow newsletter for updates on when Amber and Eric offer opportunities to travel to Emilia Romagna, to eat and drink with them!

Newsletter:

www.withhusbandintow.com/newsletter/